Legs of Lamb

Gary Lamb

New Wine Press

New Wine Ministries
PO Box 17
Chichester
West Sussex
United Kingdom
PO19 2AW

ISBN 978-1-905991-23-5

Typeset by CRB Associates, Reepham, Norfolk
Cover design by CCD, www.ccdgroup.co.uk
Printed in Malta

Contents

Foreword   7

Introduction   9

Chapter 1   Birth-pangs   11

Chapter 2   A Bolt from the Blue   23

Chapter 3   Race Against the Invisible Clock   33

Chapter 4   One More Step Along the World I Go   49

Chapter 5   The Best Laid Plans Go Where?   151

Chapter 6   Give Us Each Day   165

Chapter 7   The Heavenly Hosts!   177

Chapter 8   Having the Last Laugh   195

Chapter 9   Silence Isn't Always Golden   213

Appendix   229

Postscript   255

Foreword

"Hello. Moi nime's Gary Lame an' oim nointeen!" Friends of Gary's will perhaps recognize my poor attempt at that broad Kentish accent, but these were the first words I remember that brought Gary Lamb to my attention. The occasion was the introductory session to Gary's (and around thirty other trainees') gap year of church-based discipleship training, called DNA. It was whilst on DNA that God first spoke to this remarkable young man about prayer walking around Britain. I am responsible for the team which runs this wild, life-changing, character-crunching journey called DNA – check out our website at www.dna-uk.org.

Right from the start, Gary made an indelible and lasting impression on me, which has only been deepened after his DNA year at every subsequent opportunity I've had to serve with Gary for the sake of the Gospel of Jesus Christ. Words like "fun", "integrity", "servant-heartedness", "hard work-ing", "committed" and "teachable" spring to mind and heart when I think of Gary. And giftings like evangelist, leader, prophetic come fast behind, although God (and I!) are much more interested in who Gary is than in what he does. And this is part of the hallmark of the man. Gary is an activist (although by his own admission he can, like many of us, be lazy on occasions!) but has learned that his identity in Jesus as a son of the Father comes before his function for (or even with) Jesus. It is a profound truth we all need to keep on learning.

You are going to enjoy this book. I read a lot of books, Christian and not. Some I read because I have to, and some because I want to. Gary kindly asked me to write the foreword to this story of his adventure, so I felt I had to read it first! But "had to" quickly changed to *"wanted* to". The book is compelling, very real, very Gary. And somehow it conveys to the reader some of the life, fun and faith that Gary carries. This book will make you laugh and make you pause for thought. Sometimes you will pause for repentance and at other times because you are challenged. Throughout it Gary's humility shines through.

I have always believed in Gary, and I still do. As he stays close to Jesus, without a doubt he will go on making a difference in the lives of those around him. This book is in part a testimony to that and to the incredible releasing support that his church is. I know the church, have worked a little with them and wish there were more such churches around.

But this book is only part of Gary's story – watch this space! And as for you and me, what will we dare to dream, dare to hear, and – more than that – dare to do with God?

Enjoy!!

Pete Gilbert

Introduction

This walk "thing" all started what seems a long time ago when I was just a wee bairn. A what? Is this the real Gary Lamb using a Scots term like "wee bairn"? Born and bred in the south-east corner of Kent, isn't he the most typical user of local slang? Ha, whatever has happened to this *plastics factory worker*, or do I mean slacker? There you go, boys at VERTEX, Folkestone; I said that I would mention you in the book!

Really it all started when I was nineteen, as that strange voice that I had become accustomed to hearing down the years exploded into my conscience. *"Gary, I want you to walk around Britain."*

So why not join me on the same journey, sharing with me through my written memories of a four thousand five hundred mile trek in which I tasted a unique brew of exhilaration, disappointment, adventure, boredom, sun, wind, rain, pride and embarrassment all somehow blended together to enrich my personal walk with God?

As we move along together, walk with me across the thresholds of many wonderful homes, thrown open to me simply because I was a Christian. Find out how numerous strangers became my overnight friends. Enter into the variety of emotions which I experienced daily as yet another new location came and went.

Above all let this book encourage your faith in the God who walks through life's ups and downs with us, and who wants to be your constant lifelong walking companion. My prayer is that reading about my adventure will inspire you to follow your own heart wherever God is taking you.

CHAPTER 1

Birth-pangs

How God got into my life

Straight from the off, I didn't have a scooby of God's plans for my life, nor of – yep – more or less everything else going on around me. Even now, I only know about the first part of my journey towards God through what others have told me. In fact, during my so-called formative years, I was one of those fortunate children who never seemed to know what was happening in front of their own eyes.

Let me veer off at a tangent for a moment, so that you can take a closer look at the life and times of the young Gary. A mere four seemingly insignificant things stick in my mind from before the age of eleven, which might make some of your sides split. Firstly – remember, it must go no further than this book – there was playing pushchairs with a girl from over the road, including dolls in their full regalia! Apparently, she was besotted with me. Did I, at three, have that sort of effect on women – weak-at-the-knees, and all that? Hmmm; clearly from an early age I was destined to be popular with the ladies! By the way, if you're reading this, give me a call! Chic-a-boo, how I do miss thee! Anyway . . . my next memory is of falling from a climbing frame at the sprightly age of four. Having proudly made it to the top, I had a bit of an "I'm the king of the castle" moment! Must 'ave knocked me old thinkin' box pretty hard, as after that it all goes a bit blank, which maybe explains a few things!

Just a minute, though – it seems that two more memories remain, before the permanent blank takes over. I used to steal from my mum! It was her habit then to leave money on the sideboard. Being of such a tender, innocent age, you might think that – if the money tempted me at all – it would be in order to buy sweets for my own selfish desires. Alas; a yearning to help people clearly surfaced in me early on! Yes, I did indeed take the money from my mum, who had little enough to spare, but actually all I did was give it regularly to the School Fund! Now what would a psychologist make of that? Could it reveal a deep-rooted desire to be liked? If that is the interpretation, it would be dead right regarding me at that time! Well, the day came when the head teacher invited my mum in to thank her for generosity towards the school ... let's leave it at that, shall we?

My final childhood recollection relates to absolute heartbreak at the hands of one of my passionate loves – yes, football, of course! I was really proud of my performance in the school team, but unfortunately I always played at right back, the school "reject position". I felt that a promotion to centre of midfield was in order, but was too scared to ask the coach, who also happened to be the head teacher. So, like all brave kids of that age ... I asked my mum to speak to him. Ah, you might think, at this point I was hoping that mum's long history of generous donations to the school would give her some influence over the situation! A bit of leverage maybe!

His inability to recognize my potential astounds me to this day. Presumably, he feared that it would be too difficult for the rest of the team to accommodate a player of such a high skill level!

If it wasn't for that sad failure on my teacher's part, who knows what my future might have been? Personally, I am convinced that pro football lay just round the corner. Well, everyone has some excuse for not "making it", and that's mine.

Anyway, time to get back to my journey towards finding God. No doubt all those earliest happenings are part of His mysterious, high workings in my life. Now, allow me to draw on what mum has told me, and root around among my earlier experiences of God in action. Before I was seven, her impression was that she "didn't need God". She had just one requirement – to be loved. That's it! That is what she felt life owed her. But all was shattered, when it turned out that things had irretrievably fallen apart in her marriage to my dad. Upon this, she fell into the absolute depths of despair, actually trying suicide more than once. Then, out of the blue, God showed up for her – right in the midst of this terrible darkness. In Him she recognized and found a love deeper than anything she had ever dreamed of! And, of all things, my mum became a regular church freak!

After this encounter with God, mum made it compulsory for all of us to attend church. She used to drag us along for what seemed like an eternity, totally against our own wills. It was probably how you imagine a church to be. Pews, bells and smells, hands together, eyes closed, or at least that's how it appeared to me at the time. And – man alive! It was bitterly cold, which didn't help things. I wasn't 'avin' any of that! It's not as if I was going to put a penny in their offering bucket, for them not to invest in some quality heating! The problem lay in the fact that mum believed she was only taking us along for our benefit, whereas we couldn't stand the place. We didn't belong! There were hardly any people our age; we didn't fit in. Then, one day, when I was aged eleven, good old mum decided to ask one of her sudden questions.

To my amazement, it was simply "Gary, do you want to go to church any more?" That day for me was like going to heaven had come early. "Did I hear that right?" I asked myself. There was no way I was going back to church voluntarily! To me it was merely that cold, old building, where people used to tell me off for laughing and joking, and generally being myself. But – or so it felt – if I wore a mask, and faked a different personality that fitted in, I was acceptable, and could possibly gain the odd sweet! To my dismay, I couldn't polish off those bad boys without making a noise, so I had to wait until the end of church to tuck into those little beauts without anyone giving me the evil eye!

With hindsight, it is clear that I was *partly* to blame for my behaviour at church. Back in those days, the world still revolved around me, as clearly it should have! Hmmm... That said, let me set aside my nature to deliberately underrate myself. (I really mustn't do that.) Tail between my legs, I must admit to being more responsible for my perception of church culture than I'm letting on, although don't you think it's hard to go to church as a child, week in week out, and be told to be good *all* the time, even when the adults aren't? I've got mixed feelings about this period. Obviously, I am indebted to the Sunday school teachers for the time they invested in my life at that point. It must have been hard for them. Each week, just a couple of us would turn up and at least one – meaning myself – was a right little nightmare as well. Yet they stuck it out and – because of their faithfulness to God, and to me – I now know more about God's Word than I would have done, because they gave me the chance to listen to some of those great Bible stories as a kid. Along with that, those Sunday school teachers were praying for me. Even if nearly all their prayers during that time apparently hit heaven's ceiling, it may well be that the vital one made it through, so it was all worth it. And I honour them.

Where was I? The choice about attendance had been offered, and it hadn't taken long to make up my mind! Sundays would be mine again. Well, kinda! 'Coz it was the "Sabbath" I wasn't allowed to watch TV, play outside, or go round to the shop. But, at least church was off the menu!

After a while, however, mum herself became discontented with the status quo. She was seeking an encounter with God's

Holy Spirit, but the church that she was attending at the time didn't go for that. So – after much heartache, several lost friends, and a whole bucket-load of prayer – she felt it was time to leave. And, in a side result as yet entirely unknown to me, my second phase of church life was about to begin.

One boring Sunday, mum returned from a new church, full of beans! The home atmosphere was charged with expectancy of another up and coming question. *Oh no*, here it comes; I just know what she's going to say next! "Gary, will you go to this new church with me next week?" Sure enough, I was right; she hit me with the challenge, and it honestly felt like a painful blow from a heavyweight boxer.

Tricky one! Could this uppercut be easily dodged? I thought, "Oh well, I will go once, say I hated it, and that will get her off my back." So along I stomped, begrudgingly, and with plenty of whining.

It was different at this church, that's for sure. There were loads of young people of a similar age to mine, including some honeys. The atmosphere was surprisingly warm and welcoming. And – a completely weird idea to me at the time – they met in a school! I clearly remember thinking, "Hold on a minute; this could be quite good!" Of course, as was my custom, I ignored anything which was said from the front, and actively misbehaved at Sunday school. Yet, for some unknown reason, I came home thinking – "Those lot are OK!" Somehow, even at that age, I knew that these particular Bible-bashers were different from my group of un-churched friends. They didn't swear half as much, which is something that makes an impact on any young person that age. Nor were they as selfish as most of my mates. They actually talked to me, man! Could they be genuinely interested in me as a person?

In an age where godlessness and selfishness are continually on the increase, showing a bit of sincere interest in someone can make such a massive difference, especially when you're young. That was enough to start me attending church on a regular basis. I made some really good friends, many of whom are still great mates today. As far as I can recall at this stage of my life, the idea of a God did not interest me, nor did older people who still used to tick me off – though not quite as much at this new church! And then there were the occasional odd ones who would simply tell me that God loved me, and that they were praying for me. Those words always went right into the depths of my being, and made the hairs on the back of my neck stand on end, despite the fact that I didn't know what they were talking about. Many a Sunday was spent passing round notes to friends at church, and eating sweets on the sly. Trying to tempt younger kids to misbehave was a favourite prank of mine. A gentle tap on the shoulder would make them turn around. Then I would ignore them, until eventually they would get frustrated, and end up getting told off. Of course, I made sure to come up smelling of roses. Maybe mucking around was my way of attracting attention, due to insecurity. Having said that, I saw myself as the "cool one" amongst these cheesy Christians.

At around the age of thirteen, I went to my first youth camp, and for the very first time really listened to the message of Jesus as good news. I felt Him reaching into the very core of my heart. Many of my friends responded to the talk by raising their hands to become followers of this fella. Some of me knew what was going on, but the rest was simply copying my friends. Not wanting to be the odd one out, I stuck my own mitt in the air. I came back from the camp, having really enjoyed it, but not quite sure of what I had just committed myself to. The next couple of years tended to take the same pattern of going to a camp each summer, and making a half-hearted decision to follow this Christ. On returning home to my normal surroundings and routine, I would go through a process of feeling once again disillusioned with life, and would fall away from following Him. Was He real, or not?

For me, at that time, church was largely a social scene. Every now and again, I would say my "sorries" to a God I was not sure I believed in, and then proceed to get on with my life. It was not much of a relationship, but in some way it helped with the feeling of guilt that would now accompany me whenever I stepped out of line. I began to slip away from church life, and from my Christian friends. Occasionally I would go back, purely to see or to hang around with some of them, whilst staying firmly outside of the church. I began once again to concentrate mostly on spending more time with my other group of friends. To this day, it's hard to explain why it was. Perhaps it had to do with feeling that it was hypocritical for me to keep on going to church, whilst knowing perfectly well that no real divine connection existed. On the other hand, it may have been that I was actually choosing to love rebellion more than God.

I started to go out more at weekends, pubbing, clubbing, and generally getting totally "wasted". My friend made a fake ID because he looked so young, and I used my older brother's driving licence; we couldn't get into the clubs any other way. Getting drunk at weekends was quickly becoming a way of life. At the time there was nothing else worth doing. Whenever I got plastered, I would wake up the next morning, thinking: "All I've done is fritter away loads of money on something that was pretty rubbish."

This cruel cycle was to continue each Friday and Saturday night for another two years, whilst on Sundays I would regularly wake up sensing sharp pangs of conscience, which I chose to ignore. This felt like winning, because each occasion silenced the nagging inner voice a little bit more. And, all the time, the same thought would re-surface, buzzing around in my head . . . "There must be more to life than this!" But to me those deep questions were for somebody else to answer, and when they knew they could come and tell me. Now and again I would pop into the church service, solely to show my face.

In some bizarre way, I used to think it was a privilege for people to see me at church, especially the older folks.

Don't get me wrong. I was not really a depressed young person either. Simply being part of life used to give me a buzz, especially spending time with my family and friends. Every night, after school, we played endless games of footie down the street or numerous tournaments of ice hockey on the Sega Megadrive. We even had a top scorers' league! I used to enjoy getting into trouble, playing "knock down ginger", where you rap on a stranger's door, and then leg it. The adrenaline rush was amazing. But actually hurting people's feelings wasn't my style. I did what could be got away with, rather than going out of my way to be nasty. I had so many really cool friends who liked my way of life, and that worked!

However, this drinking habit started to bug me. I didn't like the fact that I was becoming a bit "samey". The damn thing was able to control my decisions a bit too much for my own liking. Slowly but surely, life was becoming dull, a bit of a shock because it had never been the case before. All of a sudden, the sense of fulfilment wasn't there any more. I had loved being happy, and now – emptiness. That hurt. It cut to the core of my being! Little did I know that it was all about to change. God had arranged His rescue plan for Gary Lamb.

One Sunday, I decided to attend church, and go through the normal routine of saying sorry to the God who, to my knowledge, didn't exist. (How ironic is that, by the way?) There was a guest due to speak that morning. I remember thinking, "I'll listen a bit; hope he's funny!" He started with a real classic joke, which I won't tell, in case he still uses it. Oh, go on then! He picked on Johnny, a good friend of his and our pastor at the time, who was sitting at the front of the church. I might not remember it word for word, and it won't sound half as amusing, but it really made me crease up.

"I went up to heaven and there I saw a big, long table, with guys sitting on the one side and ladies sitting facing them; it went on for miles and miles! They were all tucking in to a great banquet. You couldn't help but notice that sitting opposite me was a very attractive woman. She was amazing – tall, young, blonde, an almost perfect figure, and with a great personality. 'Does she have everything?' I thought to myself, 'God, you have done very well positioning this lady for me to look at!' Surveying the table, I noticed that people were in a particular order. Glancing down the aisle at all the blokes that I could see, I recognized some religious friends, and felt sure it must all have to do with the amount of good works they had done. If you behaved well on earth, and worked well, you got to sit opposite an attractive young lady. If you were really diligent, she would happen to be still more sensational. If, unfortunately, you didn't work so hard . . . you get the picture! Scanning the table, I became convinced that this was the case. Then I saw Johnny, looked opposite him, and almost fell off my chair.

" '*Wow!*' I thought, 'that is so not fair. She is absolutely incredible!' She was the best woman at the table, hands down. Once seen, no-one could take their eyes off her. Surely I had done far more good works than Johnny? 'That's not on,' I thought, 'God has missed a trick here!' So, I took my case up to the Almighty Himself.

" 'Hey, boss,' I said, 'this is not right! I was better than Johnny on earth. How come You've given him a more attractive woman than me? In fact, not just me, but everyone at the table?'

"The Ruler of destinies replied, 'Son, it is not for you to know why I'm punishing that poor young lady!' "

Ha, ha! Well, I thought it was funny anyway. The important thing was that it got me listening to the guy. Humour can be incredibly helpful, especially when trying to grab attention. Mine, for a change, was well and truly captured. Our guest started his message, and it was good. Then, most unusually, he stopped half way through his talk,

and made his way over towards where someone was sitting –
me! To my absolute amazement, he climbed onto a chair right
in front of Gary Lamb.

We had about two hundred people at church that morning.
He asked me to stand up, and then grabbed hold of me. Well,
how embarrassing was that? How dare this stranger man-
handle me, right in front of everyone? I had actually been
starting to like the guy as well! But, then came the defining
moment, the life-changing time. He began to speak into
my life.

The message was that God had me on a "piece of elastic".
And, no matter how far I ran away, He would keep pulling me
back and back. He mentioned the need for many years of
training and equipping. My heart started racing, and my pulse
felt heavier. I felt nervous and exposed, aware that beads of
sweat were streaming down my face. What would people
think of me? What would they say after the meeting? What
is this guy doing? Then, I allowed myself to think about
his words.

He was dead right! How did he know all that about me?
Yes, I'd been running from God, but this God had not given
up on me. Divine elastic really was hauling me in. It was not
the first time. All my life I had been around church, around
Christians, around God, but had never completely broken free
of them in my rebellion. Something always held me back, kept
me hemmed in. Things started making sense as he carried on.
He said that the hour had come to make up my mind. It was
crossroads time. Was I going to continue walking as before, or
turn in a different direction?

My heart awoke for the first time to the reality of God's
personal interest in Gary Lamb. And, on top of that, He had
homed in on me in front of all these people. All my rebellion
and sin started coming to the surface. I felt so unclean, and
knew that help was required. I needed saving, to start afresh.
The desire to be forgiven was overwhelming. A second

chance was what I desperately craved. Another crack at life, with a Friend who had power to help me live! There was a new, different road, full of surprise and adventure not seen before. I started to cry, feeling immediately self-conscious and looking around like a lost, scared rabbit that had just been blinded by car headlights. There was nowhere to run, nowhere to hide. This was it! Then, all of a sudden, came a defining moment. I thought, "Who cares if I look like an idiot, bawling my eyes out in front of these people? If God is real, then that is more important than anything else going on."

My fear of what people were thinking paled into insignificance; this was between the Maker of heaven and earth and little me, with no-one else even in the room. Guilt was confessed, and help was imminent, as God's tangible warmth surrounded me. My tiny heart was wrapped snug inside the blanket of His all-embracing love. He was there, I mean really there! Life had changed for ever. A long and exciting road lay ahead. Where would the first signpost pop up?

CHAPTER 2

A Bolt from the Blue

The vision to prayer-walk around Britain

During those next five months, my daily work pattern at the local plastic factory completely spun around. I had already managed to pull off a remarkable feat, in that the nature of my duties meant work could go on at the same time as doing other stuff, like reading the newspaper, or playing computer chess. The maximum demand of an average day's work was to cut lenses for binoculars with a hot knife, and put them into trays, which you could literally do with your eyes closed, bar a few burn marks. In addition to absorbing every detail of the sports page of my favourite tabloid, the boss and I would tackle the *Daily Mail* puzzle page for hours on end. It was our mission to defeat JUDD (the scrabble king!) which we did with a surprising amount of success. But now I could also read the Bible whilst getting on with the job, so the Scriptures more than the sports page became my number one priority. Fancy a factory worker getting paid for reading God's Word! What a unique position! Over this period, I really enjoyed my job and could plough through entire books of the Bible every day. From time to time, a mate would cover for me, and give me real stick saying, "How can you do that job? It's so rubbish!" Not for me, though. I would wake up itching to get to work. To top it all off, I had a quality boss man. We used to have great conversations about life and the Christian faith. His jokes weren't bad either!

And yet, ever since that Sunday morning when God spoke and my life changed, a longing to deepen my Christian knowledge and experience had begun to grow. Although I continued to relish being at the factory, restlessness was developing in my heart. Something else lay out there for me, and it was time to check out options for the future.

By now I was nineteen, and at this point God showed that the next stage was to take advantage of a great year out through "DNA", a Pioneer Christian-discipleship programme. Having made those couple of half-hearted decisions in my earlier teens, a more committed Christianity (not just Sundays) was a relatively new idea. DNA involved week-day study, residential training sessions, listening to lecturers on specialist subjects from around the country, home assignments, and voluntary work for the local church. This was to vary from sweeping a garden to going abroad.

On what was a run-of-the-mill course day at DNA headquarters, God's mysterious call to walk Britain's coastline was about to invade my world. As we frequently did, the course members began to worship the Lord together. Isn't it so often the case, that when we frail human beings for a single moment somehow manage to take our eyes off ourselves and fix them on God in worship, He will speak to us? Out of nowhere at all, it seemed, I sensed the Lord speaking direct to little me. Not in an audible voice, but too definitely to be ignored, or in the end to talk myself out of. To this day, long after the completion of the walk, I still occasionally need faith to believe it was the Lord's voice. His call was profound in its simplicity – no room for debate or dilution ... "Gary, I want *you* to walk *around* Britain." And then, silence!

Although the divine voice had faded away so quickly, my mind was far from still. Indeed, my thoughts were racing uncontrollably. "That was plain bizarre! Where on earth did that come from? Did I just make that up? What if I didn't? Has God Himself gone off His rocker? What will my mates think?

Gary, you've finally gone mad!" Such were my first responses. "What a strange thing to come out of the blue like that. Is this a distraction from worshipping God? Did He actually say, "I want *you* to walk *around* Britain?" Hmmm! Ever been there yourself, wondering whether God really said that?

What would you have done after such an experience? Although I thought about that inner voice a lot over the next few days, I hid everything in my heart. What was all this about?

Crucially, I was not sure about being actually willing to walk around Britain, even if it had been God's voice! You will have gathered by now that footie is my life, along with almost every active sport there is. But walking? Couldn't think of anything more lifeless! What could possibly be thrilling about your brain telling first one leg to move, then the other, time after time for no other purpose than to move at snail's pace from one place to the next? Why walk? I was the type of person who would get in the car to go for a newspaper a two-minute stroll away. The chance to slow down and appreciate creation certainly wasn't my cup of tea. Yours truly would far rather be down the pub with a few mates, downing a couple of beers and playing pool.

But, after a bit of considering, my excitement intensified at the thought of what could happen on the walk! Surely God Himself wouldn't have called me just to do a monotonous trudge around Britain? He had to have some sort of beneficial purpose behind it, didn't He? So, once again, I started to respond to the Lord with what had become the craving of my heart, since becoming a Christian. *"Lord, You know my desire is to see the reality of Your power in everyday life. Lord, I want to see miracles. I believe in You, and that You can do them. I want to be part of a generation that sees something different. I want to see change in our world. God, I'm hungry to make a difference. I'm no longer happy with everything remaining the same."*

Suddenly, every part of me felt invigorated. So what if it was only walking? With God, something that honestly seemed totally boring had the potential to become one huge adventure!

Next morning, getting ready for the early session, I vaguely recall chewing over the idea of the walk in my mind. What could God be up to? Had I simply imagined it all, or recently eaten too much cheese? Was it all a pipe dream? Could someone as ordinary as me really be a piece of the bigger jigsaw of God's purposes? While I was thinking like this, just two words – *"Matthew 10"* – came flying into my head, with a sound like an alarm bell. *"This is what your walk is about; Matthew 10!"* Being a perfect Bible scholar, I knew immediately what the passage was about. (If you believe that, you'll believe anything; my mind was a complete blank!)

Having looked it up, I found to my astonished delight that the passage totally matched my heart. The following are the verses which stood out to me, and were to become the focal point of the entire walk.

> *"He called his twelve disciples to him and gave them authority to drive out evil spirits, and to heal every disease and sickness . . . These twelve Jesus sent out with the following instructions: 'Do not go among the Gentiles or enter any town of the Samaritans. Go rather to the lost sheep of Israel. As you go, preach this message: "The kingdom of heaven is near." Heal the sick, raise the dead, cleanse those who have leprosy, drive out demons. Freely you have received, freely give . . . Whatever town or village you enter, search for some worthy person there, and stay at his house until you leave. As you enter the home, give it your greeting. If the home is deserving, let your peace rest on it; if it is not, let your peace return to you. If anyone will not welcome you or listen your words, shake the dust of your feet when you leave that home or town . . . I am sending you out like sheep among wolves. Therefore, be as shrewd as snakes and as innocent as doves.' "*   (Matthew 10:1, 5–8, 11–14, 16)

It dawned on me; I was feeling exactly as God wanted me to concerning the objective of the walk. Why? Because it was He who had sown the seeds of the vision in the fertile ground of my heart, possibly before my birth. From that day on, I often thought and prayed about what I had heard. The longing to be used by God whilst walking around Britain was never far away. Whenever I drew a little nearer to the Lord, or slowed down a bit, the idea would always return to the forefront of my mind. God did not intend me to let go of His mandate. Maybe some of you know this sort of feeling out of your own personal experience.

It would be great to say that, from this moment, I pressed forward without a wobble towards the outworking of what God had said. Again, there will be others who understand how it is that, despite every confirmation, one can doubt having really heard God's voice. In my case, I have this habit of going back and asking Him to re-state His plans and purposes for my life. Maybe I'm not alone in this! Kind of doubting Thomas-Gideon-like!

One Sunday morning, many months later, I woke up and said something like, *"Right, Lord, I need to know whether this is from You or not. I need a sign. God, if this is from you someone will say yes. I need to know today! I have been thinking about this walk for too long now."* It so happened that Paul, a leader from a Maidstone church, was our guest speaker that morning. However, he knew nothing about the voice; in fact, no-one did at that point. At the end of the meeting, he simply came up to me and uttered these words – *"God says, 'Yes'."* Then he left in a puff of smoke, without saying anything else!

Immediately, I was on cloud nine. God had used another person to re-emphasise His intention to send me on this walk. Hardly able to contain myself, I was shaking whilst drinking my cuppa. Paul's words had stirred faith in my heart to continue pushing forward.

Some time later, I asked the Lord for another sign, going off to sleep on this prayer – *"Please speak to me, Lord, **about** the walk."* What I was really after was starting to put some bones on the vision. Everything was still too fuzzy for me. On waking next morning, the words *"Fifteen miles a day, six days a week for about a year"* kept repeating themselves in my head. Unusually, what I had been dreaming all night was still alive in my head. I had no concept of their exact meaning, but knew the figures must be related to the walk. Still wondering about it all, I entered them into a calculator, taking a year as 52 weeks, and came up with the total of 4,680 miles. A quick check on the internet showed that 4,680 miles was the necessary walking distance needed in order to do a basic round-Britain coastal walk within a year. *Wow!* No room for coincidence there! The Lord had heard my prayer, and was starting to give me His direction for the basic structure of the walk. Don't you love it when a plan comes together?

Again (as you do), I continued to ask for confirming signs. This time, it was another visiting speaker. His name was Tim, and he is not so much older than I am. I asked him to pray for me personally, but didn't tell him why. I'd said to God, "Please can this man pray about the walk that You want to send me on?" When Tim, quite naturally, asked if my request for prayer was a response to his message, my reply came, "No, but can you just pray whatever comes into your head?"

His words went something like this: "Lord, as Gary *travels* on his *journey*, I pray he will know where he is *going*, and that You will put *signposts* where he needs them. Each *step* that he takes, may You *walk* with him." Tim continued using this type of journeying phraseology throughout his prayer. Again, God had responded patiently to my demand for another sign!

My inner confidence that this was a true call from God continued to grow. As previously mentioned, though (I'm not going to lie to you!), I'm still prone to doubt. Yes, even though I have seen and heard so much, and am now sitting with my laptop writing this book after completing the walk, my faith is still challenged. Doubt is a battle we Christians come up against on a continual basis. But now, enough had happened for me to believe that God's go-ahead was real. It was time for a few more people to know about the vision and to start thinking about a firm date. After chatting to my friends about the idea, a few expressed so much interest that I began to dream of a group project. Carrying tents, cooking our own meals under the stars, singing round a camp fire of a night, and taking the British coastline by storm! Whack! All that line of thinking became an impenetrable wall; and what I assumed to be God's designs turned out to be simply random bricks of my own thoughts.

It was at this stage that I also felt the time had come to ask my church elders to definitely back the vision for the walk, and to be alongside me as I began to make preparations. By a God-incidence, it turned out that they had already decided that it was right to encourage me, by making time and opportunity available. If this was to take off, it would need their backing, which I'd been unsure about, since more than one of them had previously expressed reservations and practical concerns. As you can imagine, I was worried about whether they would now share my increasing sense of urgency. Would they still doubt my ability to do what I was certain God had told me to do, or not support the idea simply because of uncertainty? My thoughts were racing now. The elders might come on board, but would the whole church back me? What about my family, what would they think? How would I manage without them? Was it possible for me to survive a whole year without playing football? It was unthinkable! Wouldn't I miss my friends too much, especially going to the pub with them for a pint? Could the church find replacements to fill the various gaps which would be left, in terms of leadership roles amongst the youth and children in particular? What about all the friendships built with everyone over the years? How could I maintain them? Would it be possible to do so, or would I be bound to lose some? The potential loss of a single one seemed too much of a sacrifice.

Time had flown by, and it was nearly six years since I had heard God's voice that day. To say I was in a hurry to get walking would be an understatement. It wasn't clear what would happen, or how things might work out. Yet I was just so, so sure that God had spoken to me!

However, on meeting up with the elders, I was somewhat surprised and extremely grateful to find that God had also spoken clearly to them, and that they were now ready to swing fully into support. Their generosity was going to extend to allowing other staff to help with planning and preparing. And I came away from that meeting with the new and invaluable idea of setting up a couple of trials, so that stamina, strength and perseverance could be tested, and informed views acquired about what I would need to take with me. Perhaps behind their decisions lay the thought that it would be good for me to go through the preliminary process of walking fifteen miles alone, dealing with blisters, navigating, living out of a rucksack, and at the same time praying and reaching out, before committing myself to the full project.

The green light had been given, but was I ready to hit the gas, or was I still stuck in neutral? What had been purely a pipe-dream for the past six years was about to become an actuality. How would I be able to cope with that?

Also, one by one, my group of buddies had realized that God's voice to me didn't apply to them, and they wouldn't be coming with me. Though still conscious of the support of family, some close friends and the elders, I couldn't help feeling alone, perhaps a bit like Gideon did when God first asked him to do something beyond his natural ability, and then trimmed his army. My reliance now had to shift from me to God. Ever since becoming a Christian I had claimed to trust Him. Would that call prove to be genuine, or mere words? God had smashed a huge gaping hole through my force field, and walked through it ahead of me. But was I ready and equipped to follow?

So far, it's been pretty obvious that I'm a bit of a slow learner. It gradually dawned on me that it is possible to hear God's voice clearly, but still add on your own extras, to say nothing of others kindly adding in their own contributions! Take Abraham, for example. He heard God's voice about as clearly as you possibly can – angels and the works! It came with a specific promise, saying: "I will give you more descendants than the number of stars in the sky." But, after something like ten years, his wife Sarah had still failed to conceive, so they decided to do it their own way, not how God had planned things. As a result, Abraham sinned badly and fathered a son through his wife's servant Hagar, rather than waiting for God's best. Although he got it wrong, God did not treat him the way the world might have done. There is no divine rubbish heap! Instead, He still wanted to continue His original grand plan. Abraham and Sarah *were* to produce a son of their own – some might say not a moment too soon!

I suppose I'd fit that in a way – not that I'm planning to wait until one hundred before my (hopefully) future wife gives me a child. But hey – guess it's not my plans that will count! Like Abraham, I had added my own details to God's blueprint. Don't you think it's quite amazing that God still chooses to work through us, even when we put our dirty fingers on His sovereign designs? In my case, it had become all about my views, and the way forward that seemed obvious to me. God was just the back-seat driver who I didn't listen to, and there was room for other passengers.

Allow me to jump back to chapter 1. Remember how it was mentioned that there would be "many years of instruction and training"? If only I had taken those original words into consideration before trying to work out my own plan of campaign. It would have saved me a lot of unnecessary brain-ache. I wasn't thinking much about being instructed or trained. I'd heard the call, but overlooked the detail. God didn't intend this to continue, and He clearly started to work on the hearts of others who knew me.

From among the team of elders who had been such a blessing in my life, God chose to place alongside me a man by the name of Vincent Oliver, who was already investing his time and life into mine. We had worked alongside each other a lot over a five-year period. Anyway, virtually everything I knew about God's voice to me regarding the walk, the V-man knew. One day, as he was sitting reading Matthew 10, a verse that hadn't seemed too significant to me suddenly stood out to him. It was verse 11: *"Whatever town or village you enter, search for some worthy person there, and stay at his house until you leave."* God wasn't saying anything about tents after all! This was not a totally unwelcome revelation! Instead, He wanted me to stay in homes from place to place around the British coastline. Nice!

CHAPTER 3

Race Against the Invisible Clock

The vision comes together

That mysterious voice I was now banking everything on had spoken – the period of training was well under way. It was time for the nuts and bolts. A walk of this magnitude does not just fall into your lap! I'd read enough books on the subject to know that much. It was hardly encouraging to find that almost every single one referred to a stress fracture to the foot (ouch). That wasn't all, either! Other potential horrors lay ahead of me: blisters, uncomfortable nights, extreme weather conditions – sunburn and soggy maps, periodic attacks of clegs and midges (the unique Scottish speciality). Not to mention the possibility of being trapped by incoming tides, experiencing hunger pangs or getting utterly lost. Ironically, my sense of direction is so bad I sometimes get lost within half a mile of home! How about wearing out of innumerable and quite "cheesy" socks, walking in the dark, sinking in the bogs, disastrous shortage of toilet facilities, along with all the other dangers lurking around the corner, of which I was unaware? It had become clear by now that for most of the time I would be literally on my own. So some very careful, detailed advance planning was going to be needed, and the sooner the better.

Perhaps the best way to start was to get on and do those couple of trial walks. That way I would know what I didn't know. I'm very modest about my quite remarkable physique, hmmm, so the strenuous test of a practice walk in the mountains of either Scotland or Snowdonia, or the steep climbs of North Devon didn't seem quite enough. Instead, the hero in me demanded the notoriously harsh inclines of the flattest lands in England, and I chose to face up to the unbearable challenge of a five-day wander around the Fens.

This brief adventure was also a good opportunity to test Vincent's insight into Matthew 10. How practical would it really be? Could there in fact be people who were willing to risk taking an intruder into their homes for a night? My disqualifications seemed too numerous to count. I was distinctly aware of being young, tall, good looking (had to get that in) and male, which is not always an advantage when meeting strangers for the first time – except with kind old ladies, of course! Would they see me as a bit of a yobbo, and someone who was about to steal their gear? Having a laddish Kentish accent, along with speaking all that Lambese rather than the Queen's English, didn't exactly help matters. My lack of general knowledge often gets me into deep doodoo at Hythe's local pub quiz. What if my hosts wanted to talk about anything other than God or football? Would I be able to relate on the level that might be expected of me? My home church has a very informal style, and gives emphasis to friendship and "family". Might that be a hindrance to Christians from different traditions or backgrounds? In fact, how many hosts of any kind would warmly welcome the unappetizing stench that – after a hot day's walk – would inevitably accompany me through their front door? Food for thought, eh!

So, two outright beginners began the process of selecting appropriate locations in the hope of finding accommodation to match. It transpired that Vincent had a bit more personal experience of those flat-landed Fens than I had realized. He had only gone and arranged for Joe (one of his billion of brothers) to move out there thirty years ago, exclusively for my benefit! But one of the things Vincent has often given it the large about is that things seem to simply happen for me, in situations where other people might have to get on and put in a bit of personal hard graft and sweat. So it was with a sort of optimistic shrug that he got in touch with Joe, and set the ball rolling. Between the three of us, a route was sorted that would take me from Crowland to Wisbech, Holbeach, Boston, Bourne, and finally back to Deeping St James.

It was time to apply Matthew 10. Joe had very kindly organized two nights' accommodation for me, but the other three were down to us. Thankfully, our church office included among its resources an annual publication known as *The Body Book*. It is produced by Pioneer People, and is basically a list of churches similar in nature to our own, which meant that we could have at least some confidence about making an out-of-the-blue approach. In the long run, we were to find the book of fairly limited help when it came to finding accommodation right round the coast, but it was fine for now. As a result, Wisbech and Boston quickly became pretty good options, thanks to a positive response from two extremely friendly ministers. All we had for Holbeach was a possible contact, but we decided to push the boat out and believe that something would come good on the day. We were ready to roll!

Things went fine with everything that Joe and his family had generously set up. Comfy double beds, wonderful meals, great people, the kind of street conversational opportunities I had been longing for – I could get used to this! However, I was to learn that even a walk done for God doesn't necessarily run smoothly. Holbeach was a pleasant enough place, but the accommodation plans started as uncertain, and finished up as non-existent. Having bottled out on the pre-planned altern-ative of a faith-filled roadside kip for the night, and after numerous efforts to find somewhere cheap in a hurry, my day there ended in a pretty swanky hotel. An expensive £59 lesson to be learned quickly – I couldn't afford too many repeats of such pricey stopovers. But I had long enough to envision future millionaire sponsors who would insist on funding five-star hotels throughout the main walk. Yes, in my dreams each day would then start with a massage, full mud pack, facial make over, a leg wax (maybe not . . .) and a manicure, before I set off. Each evening, the senior hotel manager would greet me personally with a Chardonnay, before escorting me to my private VIP suite fully equipped with sauna, steam room, jacuzzi and (of course) a four-poster king-sized bed. I find being alone in one of those gives me enough room to really express myself. Enough of the dreaming!

Come on now . . . there were other aspects to be trialled, as well as accommodation. The Fens taught me a lot. I became aware that really satisfactory footwear would be needed, as well as clothing, means of carrying gear, first-aid kit, route-finding materials, and personal safety equipment. For some reason, I had thought it would be fine to wear lightweight, non-breathable (phew!) trainers right around Britain, so that's all I took to the Fens. I would definitely need some of those fancy hiking boots!

As for keeping dry, it took just one day of a Fenland February downpour to teach me that my budget Regatta waterproofs would not be up to the job. And, boy, did it rain – cats and dogs! It was the sort of weather Noah would have been impressed by! Nor did I know then that a couple of flimsy black bags inside a rucksack would do the trick for keeping my clothes at least semi-dry. If anyone wants to ask whether my cheap-skate pretence of a rucksack provided adequate shoulder support – that's best left unwritten about! But the answer was to be etched into my shoulders for days on end.

Joe had gone the extra mile, in providing me with daily printed route maps. But his well-meant plastic A4 pockets could not protect them from the onslaught of the particularly fierce Fenland felines and canines I have just mentioned! All of which was going to need mulling over. How many maps would I need to take with me in order to find my way right around Britain, and how on earth would I keep them dry? Where would I buy them, or how could I organize the expensive task of having someone post them to me as needed? Blisters I was resigned to, so the real surprise was not that I got them, but that they so badly caned my lower extremities! It seemed that being an addictive footballer was no preparation for what I was about to undertake, so far as my poor feet were concerned.

Vincent and many others have been known to say that my belly is a close rival with football when it comes to lordship. Who knows whether that is a joke? What I can say for sure is that after a couple of hours' walk each morning I was ready to eat several large, fleshy Shire horses. It didn't matter how big a breakfast had been provided by my more than generous hosts. By 11 o'clock I would feel physically knackered, and would be audibly aware of a dissatisfaction within my stomach. Nosebag was the sole remedy for this serious craving. I learned that part of my early morning routine would need to be stocking up with supplies of grub. My alarm bells rang again, this time with regard to the expense of the forthcoming major walk. I hadn't bargained for needing two lunches a day! Anyway, at the end of the week, I came home with a bit of experience and exercise under my belt, along with a whole load of pies. But now, I was all too aware of needing to learn a whole bucketful more from the second anticipated trial walk. I had made a start though, and enough good things had happened to show that we were by no means talking Mission Impossible.

Now that I had cut my teeth in the kindergarten of my first trial walk, it was time to move up to the reception class. The welcoming wineglass was empty, and I felt ready to order the starter. My second practice was already planned for the height of the summer, among the hills of Devon. No, I wasn't out solely to get a sun-tan for two weeks. For the next four months I was champing at the bit, impatient to paw the red ground of Devon. Eventually, the due day arrived, and I took myself west. Despite the fact that I drove my bogey green Hyundai Accent, the journey was quite straightforward. This may come as a surprise to Jeremy Clarkson, especially in the light of the fact that I overtook a good number of tractors. *Top Gear*, eat your heart out!

I can only say that the demands of the West Country were somewhat greater. The walk went from a mere five days to a more challenging nine, from freezing rain to baking sun, from a gentle stroll around the Fens to the steep inclines of the South West coastal path which were to find out every weak muscle in my skinny pins. My route started and ended at Dartington, and embraced Torquay, Dawlish, Exeter, Exmouth (twice), Ottery St Mary, Chard and Lyme Regis, each day's walk being between ten and twenty miles.

Accommodation arrangements took a similar pattern to the previous trial, although we were careful to start planning earlier this time. For all we knew, Devon hotels might have been yet more expensive, and we didn't want to get stung again. The schedule included an intentional unplanned night in Torquay, and this time the faith approach was vindicated, since with just twenty-four hours to go a totally unexpected option emerged. I was to spend a quality evening with new Christian friends from Project 58 (a drugs rehab centre). As before, all my hosts were top-drawer in their practical and spiritual care for me. I also caught a few initial glimpses of what were to be common strands for the future main walk. Firstly, that each day was likely to end with invitations to speak at a local group, and to share about my vision and my faith. Secondly, that Christians who undertake to offer hospitality overnight to a stranger from Kent certainly do so in style. The Bible might talk about simply offering a cup of cold water in the name of Jesus, but these guys gave me the full works in terms of a sumptuous late afternoon meal on arrival and – before I could even walk off the effects – a scrumptious early morning cooked brekkie! I am certainly no angel, but they did entertain me well, in Hebrews 13:2 style.

One thing I'd not experienced in the Fens was dehydration! But, in the South West, in June, it didn't seem to matter how much fluid I consumed. Apparently, I had an invisible leak. Then there was the continual irritation of having to take off my rucksack, in order to access my water supply. I had two pint-sized bottles for a six-hour walk, which in my ignorance I thought would be more than sufficient. What a donkey! They were both emptied each day within an hour of starting out, and I had to keep buying whenever I saw a shop. Oh well – more holes in the wallet maybe – but also more useful lessons for a future which was to include walking whole days (in North Scotland particularly) without ever coming within sight or sound of any kind of shop, short of hallucination.

Probably most of us have our own opinions of the man notoriously named "The Naked Rambler", but I began to understand a little bit of the way he might feel sometimes. How anybody can possibly survive long midwinter walks outdoors without a radiator in their coat baffles me. But this was a tad different. Day after day, I was down to merely a pair of shorts – of suitable decency, naturally! It was too damn hot to tolerate any more clothes. The macho in me wasn't interested in things like sun-cream, but this experience quickly revealed that I needed to focus on more important priorities than the personal vanity of acquiring a good sun tan. The sun was burning my skin, and it really hurt, especially around the rucksack straps. You might wonder how come I was about to turn twenty-five and hadn't cottoned on to that one? Hmmm!

Ah yes, the rucksack! By now I was sure that I needed something with more shoulder padding, greater general capacity, and kinder back support for my future walk. It's hard to remember now how very little I knew then about the different kinds of purpose-built rucksacks, and I was beginning to realize that cheap wasn't necessarily cheerful! Putting aside enough finance for buying purpose-made equipment would be essential.

Intense sunburn, unquenchable thirst, painful shoulder-strain, never-ending hunger pangs, as well as uncertainty about where I would lay my head of a night, were issues that began to play on my mind. Yet nothing had prepared me for the sense of outright fear for the entire future of the walk which was about to cast its shadow. Physical fitness was something I had always taken for granted – but no longer! About three days from the end of this second trial, as I was simply walking up yet another hill, I felt an excruciating pain at the back of my lower right leg, close above the heel. My football expertise (which I have already mentioned so often that it is becoming a touch sad) meant I kind of knew it was my Achilles tendon. Aware that this was not going to be a quick-fix matter, I finally tried phoning back to base, and got some common sense advice. I had to stock up with strong painkillers, and strap up heavily in order to continue. Unknown to me, this was the best immediate treatment, and over the rest of the day the agony eased slightly. With God's help, I was able to enjoy the rest of my time walking through the ongoing pain of the remaining three days, but this new dilemma was now permanently stamped on my memory. Of my spiritual inadequacy I had long been convinced, but the notion of being unable to meet the physical demands of the walk was revolutionary – and scary.

However, by His grace, God transformed the discouragement into a still stronger resolve to pursue my vision for the walk. Not long afterwards a start date was agreed with my church elders, and with this in mind I became aware of an urgent need to work more regularly on my physical toughness. It was time to beef up those scrawny limbs. How do you balance that with a full-time job, even if it is for a church? To begin with, my training had to be done before work started, which was usually no later than 8.30 a.m. since my duties included participating in early morning school assemblies.

As my alarm sounded each day around 6.30 a.m., I was like a fat slug, glued to my blanket with the slime of sleepy unwillingness to get up. No-one could have described me as a rising salmon full of joyful anticipation of the adventures of the new day to come. It would be difficult to recount what on earth happened on those pre-dawn adventures, since to this day I'm convinced I was virtually sleepwalking. God must have done a few miracles to keep me safe from the hazards of early morning Michael Schumachers, as they roared along the A259 racetrack, or from slipping down into the clutches of those grey, entangling weeds which choke the Hythe canal. Not to mention the tidal waves of the roughest coastal stretch in Britain – maybe not! Someone, somewhere must have known that it was time to eliminate the increasing risk element, or perhaps they couldn't help noticing the less than attractive encrustation which was beginning to encircle and weigh down my poor eyes.

Having said all that, funnily enough it came about that I started to do my walking later on in the day. With just three months to go, it was time to step up a gear in terms of distance and physical demand. Instead of being satisfied with five miles on the level, there was a need to increase everything in every way – distance, weight, incline, time, and terrain. Of course all this had implications as to my availability for normal duties, but I knew I had the encouragement and active support of the whole church in pursuing this higher level of preparation. As soon as the funds became fully available, Vincent and I started to intrude more frequently on work life with regular trips to the Army Surplus shop, Tog 24, Mountain Warehouse and the like. We tried to buy all the things that I needed to upgrade, and those I had learned about through the trial walks and the advice of my newly formed support group. This became a really useful talking point when we were doing schools' visits, as I would take along my stuffed rucksack and get the children to guess what was inside, before finally revealing the contents to their dazzled gaze. A bivouac bag was purchased for those future glorious nights which I fondly imagined spending under the stars. Testing this bag in all weather conditions before I left was deemed 100% essential.

By now my afternoons were largely spent thinking through the practicalities of my schedule. One thing surfaced early on in our plans – the need to build in Sundays as practical (washing clothes, planning route, sorting rucksack, etc.) and spiritual refreshment times, plus an extra twenty-four hours every third week to sort myself out and recharge my batteries. When the idea of including a home visit every six weeks came up, I was originally mulish, and Vincent still remembers our somewhat heated debates on the matter. He felt that it would be an essential part of keeping the church on-board, as well as providing me with necessary unwinding time. With extreme unwillingness I gave in, and began to plan how this idea might work out. My well-advertised reluctance turned to enthusiasm, as I discovered that the potential mid-May break would enable me to attend a friend's wedding, the one in late June would coincide with my birthday, and the mid-August possibility would facilitate participation in the church youth camp, one of my favourite annual treats.

I had seen myself as a clone Spiderman who would easily undergo transformation into the strong, silent, self-sufficient type, you know, the sort of guy who lets go of everything to take on the world. But it only took the above to dispel all my illusions. Whilst developing my latent skills in mastering the combination of old-fashioned map-reading and twenty-first-century computerized route-finding. I learnt rather a lot very quickly in relation to names of towns I had never heard of, for example Altandhu or Penzance (!). And names like Merioneth, Denbigh, Monmouth or Pembroke (!) were totally new to me. Come on, be honest; did you know they were all Welsh counties? We could also foresee a number of points where suitable destinations at appropriate distances from one another in Scotland would be unlikely. Never before had I realized that there exists a considerable part of the United Kingdom where even hamlets – let alone villages – can be separated by twenty miles or more. What I was really looking for were well-spaced towns at regular, civilized intervals, where Vincent could optimistically search for a host church. Maps and I had never really mixed before, but from this time forward we would become inseparable companions.

What I'm trying to say is that everything was hotting up, as the church office began to overflow with all the stuff connected to my mission. Not a single day passed in those last two months before 1st April without something pretty significant happening in terms of getting sorted for the walk.

The last Sunday arrived, when the church was to formally send me out as a son of South Kent Community Church (SKCC), going from them, but at the same time remaining part of the family, and expecting to return. I was really surprised at how emotional and tearful I felt, as I stood with my family at the front of the church, looking out at two hundred and fifty friends all rooting for me, as they had been doing for quite some time. It was hard to concentrate on what was said. Everything seemed a bit of a dreamlike blur. But this was the beginning of the realization of what I had wanted for so long. All that was being so lovingly expressed was totally accurate, but in my mind I had already started the walk, whilst my uninhabited body remained the focus of everyone's attention. It would have made great ammunition for those who were close to me, who know that from time to time (shall we say) my brain goes into "back-in-five-minutes" mode. In fact, some church folk will have found this out for the first time right now. All I know is that I still felt my heart beating in the almost tangible warmth of their love. Fortunately a church family grub session followed immediately, and

as usual my brain cells revived in tandem with the stuffing of
an immense bit of nosebag into my ever ready and willing
food barrel. Game on! Eventually, after some relatively sane
chinwags, I came away knowing that the starter's whistle had
been blown. The marathon was about to begin. Next time I
attended my home church, it would be on the back of six
weeks' worth of the up and downs of walking Britain's shores.

A few final panic-stricken purchases punctuated those last
four days. Due to my idleness, some really important things
just didn't happen. A gentlemanly way of putting it would be
to say that "due to a unique and unforeseeable combination of
circumstances, the desired result unfortunately and unavoid-
ably failed to materialize". Come on, gentlemen, excuses are
like armpits – we all have them, and they stink! This is simply
a long, drawn out way of sneakily confessing that I chickened
out of my remaining opportunities to test my still untouched,
spanking new, super-costly bivvy bag investment. Vincent
had long since given up reminding me about it, having found
out a certain truth over the years. What could that be? Just
that for me it is often particularly true about the spirit being
willing, but the flesh shamelessly and wilfully weak. As he
knows to his cost, this is generally due to a unique and un-
mouldable combination of Lambishness and laziness. I told
myself it was right to wait. My reasoning was that in future a
strong desire to use my new bag would inevitably emerge
from somewhere. When it did, always assuming the weather
was OK, I would naturally reject even a definite offer of
luxurious five-star accommodation, along with a gut-buster
of a meal from potential hosts, in favour of a night in the
wild with the rats for company and the ration pack for my
main course.

A time might come – my dreams went on – when I would
face the one true test ... extreme weather conditions, surrounded by unimaginable hostile animals representing a more
worthwhile challenge to my caveman wit. My knowledge of

history was shaky, to say the least, so I was less than sure about wolves and bears having been extinct in this country for over five hundred years. Were tarantulas really only to be found in cages, or would they be lying in wait to penetrate my bivvy bag beside some remote Scottish loch? Hopefully, I wouldn't wake up one icy morning trapped in my bivvy, sliding to my fate in the jaws of the notorious Nessie! In actual fact, I had more than once dreamt that I would be carried off – bivvy bag and all – by the local refuse van, and allocated for appropriate recycling.

And so April Fools' Day 2005 eventually dawned. I spent the previous night getting all the gear crammed into the rucksack (including the unused bivvy bag). To call it a tight fit would be an understatement, and – man alive! – did it feel heavy when I slung it on to my shoulders! I can't remember dreaming, but I woke many times during the night hazily wondering what an earth I was getting myself into.

Vincent had arranged a central meeting point for anyone who was free to come and see me take my position at the starting blocks. I had offered my chum the sun a chance to come and see me off in person that morning, and he duly obliged – shooing away every trace of cloud. No doubt this was in order to give himself the best possible view, as well as to bring an extra sparkle to the waves on my right. Considering it was a run-of-the-mill working day, I was astonished and majorly heartened at the sight of so many friends and family from all walks of life who had gathered at Stade Court Hotel, Hythe, to sound the starter and cheer me off. I found myself wondering what the early morning joggers thought of this hubbub of excited voices, and the brandishing of colourful banners by several well-wishers.

Despite having lived by the sea for twenty-one years, I have to say that I had never really valued it until that first day. As I considered its awe-inspiring vastness, I realized that it would become more than a companion, and would rarely be out of sight. Just occasionally, I might have walked beside it in the past, but never with any depth of appreciation. By way of an April Fool wisecrack, I had deliberately set out by walking a few yards with the sea on my left! As I turned around, it flashed through my mind that for many months its presence on my right would be God's guiding provision.

At least twenty friends accompanied me for the first two-mile shoreline stretch, as the dream ultimately turned into reality. From this moment forward, my brain would be sending thousands of identical signals to my legs each day. In response, those elongated extremities would mechanically place themselves one in front of the other to create steps. Repeated often enough, steps would become miles, of which each would count towards the fifteen which were to make up my average dose for the next three hundred and seventeen days.

No sooner had my beloved friends and family disappeared from sight, than I felt it necessary to preserve my stamina by off-loading my kitchen sink (otherwise known as my rucksack) onto Dan's poor shoulders. That monstrosity of a bag would become a part of me for the next ten and a half months, but I was more than happy to postpone the moment, especially as I looked over at Dan, quite bowed down under its weight! It dawned on me that for the foreseeable future I myself could well be perceived by everyone I met as a poor relation of the Hunchback of Notre Dame. Already I was beginning to wonder if once again I had overrated my now bulging shoulder-muscles. That thought was to recur more insistently over the next few days.

By the end of those first two miles, my walking companions had reduced to three, as the demands of the daily grind called many elsewhere. Sam, Dan (still staggering under my rucksack) and Francoise soldiered onwards for a further three miles, during which we began to get down to the business of praying. God would be hearing more from me than He had for a while ... but for now it was time to stop off at the familiar family home in Folkestone. Here an extra treat awaited Sam (now on rucksack duty and sweating heavily) and myself, having said goodbye to Francoise and Dan.

> "First day, exciting! First of many steps protected and led by God, each a step of faith!"
>
> **Francoise**

Now came the real wrench; after some nosh, and one of those cuppas that only my mum makes, came the final tearing away from everything I was used to.

So much more was to happen throughout that eventful first day. In Capel le Ferne Dan rejoined us for another couple of miles (and a second lunch!), bringing with him Nathaniel, Andrew and his mate Mark. We were ready to put prayer to the test, and we specially asked God to send someone who needed physical healing into the all but empty café. Well, He did His bit, as always! Almost immediately a challenging prayer opportunity arrived. No, it wasn't a small child with a bruised knee, in need of a fake plaster to reassure him that everything would be OK. Through that café door, bent over and dependent on the support of sticks, came God's answer to our request – a lady in desperate need. We looked at her, then at each other, and we knew what the Lord wanted us to do. But neither of us spoke nor did anything: we simply chickened out!

God later on graciously gave us a couple of really good witnessing opportunities, first with the owner of the café, then with another random walker, but we knew in our hearts that we missed part of plan A for the day. I find it amazing that He eternally chooses to forgive and forget our inability to actively obey, and grants us more chances. He does not disqualify us for future service purely because we have messed up once, or even more often.

And so to Dover, and the first of many nights to come which were to be spent under the welcoming roof of a Christian family. Gary, Tracey and their five quality kids are part of my church, and this made it so much easier to relax. Despite the misgivings of several friends, it seemed I could indeed manage to find my way using the GPS. At this point it was by the skin of my teeth, however! I had yet to realize its accuracy, and that it didn't need my "brainwork" to help it out! I sat on my sofa bed, wrote my first day's record into my phone, and sent it to the walk website.

Although I had enjoyed a good long soak in the bath, and a tasty meal, I was extremely conscious of aches and pains all over, especially in my feet. As I struggled to sleep after the excitement of that first day, I began to sense that I had just begun an epic that would need to include amazing provision, time to really talk to God and daily encounters with ordinary people. I could see that I would need consistent home base support, sympathetic hosts, charged up GPS and phone etc. Would each day's route be as challenging as the first? Would the weather be kind? Would my back hold out under the weight of that rucksack? What about those nasty blisters? What coincidences (or God-incidences) might lie ahead? The possibilities and uncertainties spun endlessly in my mind, and I fell asleep with most of them unresolved.

CHAPTER 4

One More Step Along the World I Go

Life on the road

In order to keep this chapter from rivalling the Bible in length, I have had to cut short a number of stories, and have not been able to mention details about every last town, village, hamlet etc. Hosts – I'm really sorry if you are not mentioned! I've chosen to go for a more brief account of daily experiences, rather than writing lots on particular days, to include as many areas as possible. As you read, you may find yourself crying out for more depth and feeling; don't worry, you will find it in the chapters to come. Occasionally, you will find specific days which made more of an impact. For those days I have written more, and even touched here and there on a bit of the history that I picked up on as I travelled – not that I could be tested on it now without detailed notes!

The first six weeks saw me get from Hythe to Hartlepool. If you were to carefully examine a map, you might think that doing so much in such a short space of time means I could have had the whole walk done and dusted in a maximum of six months, since this stint seems to include such a relatively big chunk of the English coastline. But, as they say, "don't judge a book by its cover". I knew that I'd done slightly less than six hundred of the four and a half thousand miles required to complete the entire loop. This period, although it did not necessarily contain the most fantastic scenery or the most exciting adventures, was nevertheless the start of the fulfilment of a dream. So I've decided to write about each place in the period up to my first home break.

Sandwich, Herne Bay, Sittingbourne, Maidstone, Gravesend = 81 miles

As early as the second day, a record was set that was not to be broken throughout the walk. At the start of the journey towards Sandwich, four-year-old Toby, plus Dad (Gary May) and older brothers Jonathan and Daniel managed to pull off a mile for every year of his life (without much help). This made him the youngest of all my walking companions, apart from one or two nippers in buggies later on. Good on ya, buddy! In fact, it was to be a day of more firsts, and less bottling out. We met and prayed for a lady in the Christian bookshop who had leg ligament problems – and who was more than grateful. It's amazing that most people are perfectly happy to be prayed for, regardless of whether they believe in God or not.

My camera came out and snapped away, as we saw the wonderful white cliffs of Dover which had always only been a few miles from my house, but until that moment sadly unappreciated by one Gary Lamb! We stopped off at the first of what was to be well over three hundred pubs in total. I sank my first pint of lager – which hardly touched the sides of my dry mouth. To be honest, I could have stayed there, on that bench, enjoying the sun all day. But we had to plod on; my next hosts were awaiting my arrival.

For the first time, I was to stay with and relate to complete strangers. The fear barrier was broken, and in just a few minutes I felt like part of their everyday furniture. I'm known to forget the odd thing or two, so when Amy twice invited us to tuck in I had to conceal a smirk, because – though the dinner was arranged perfectly on the table – there were no plates to eat from. It was the kind of prank a mate might pull off deliberately, to frustrate the groanings of the Lamb belly. Did

Amy already know me that well? Derek, Amy and the children really helped me to feel at home, and be myself on this, the first of so many weekends to come, when I would be away from friends, family and football. For the second night running, I slept like a log, and was so tired I didn't want to get up. The luxurious double bed and its fresh, clean sheets clung on to my already tired body. That Sunday, as if by a God-incident, the preacher (Derek) was speaking about recognizing Jesus when He is walking with you along the road of your life. It was the perfect preach at the start of this marathon to come!

During the next few days I was going to have to divert slightly inland, in order to achieve a Thames crossing at Gravesend. In Herne Bay I witnessed what seemed to be the biggest DVD collection in history, which Don and Mary let me take full advantage of as I watched *The Incredibles* followed by *The Matrix*, well into the early hours. Next morning, I awoke feeling like a super hero all over again – ready to take on the world.

As the sea slowly disappeared beyond my sight I felt alone, and the fear of getting lost increased. I hadn't realized that I'd been watching it for the last few days, nor that its presence had been a calming reassurance. Whilst staying in Sitting-bourne, I drooled over watching Liverpool smash Juventus in the Champions' League. What a result, and I was able to watch it! A meeting was due that night and had to be called off for some reason! As you can imagine, this didn't bother me too much; I even dared to believe that it was God's grace to me.

In Maidstone my kind hosts gave me a packed lunch so huge that it lasted an entire three days – bonus! Whilst inching slowly but surely towards Gravesend, and showing off by reading *Pilgrim's Progress* as I walked, I chanced to look up at the very moment of passing a road sign. Guess what it said? "Pilgrims Way" – cool! Talk about being in the right place at the right time. As I neared the town, I had to urgently answer a question which the children had asked several months earlier, back at Palmarsh School – where they say it as it is.

"Gary, what will you do, if you need to go for a pooh on your walk?" All I can say is, "Thank God for quiet woods and large leaves!" Soon after that empty-out, I paid the penalty for crossing a field illegally, when a herd of wild horses came charging in my direction and sent me over a nearby fence at lightning speed. I can't remember for sure, but my impression is that I needed another immediate stop-off at the woods as a result!

Westcliff-on-Sea, Wickford, Maldon, Colchester = 51 miles

In Westcliff-on-Sea I met Idy, and had the amazing answer to prayer that you can read about in chapter 6. Young Rhiannan, one of Wickford's more exciting inhabitants, re-christened me Barry there. She also gave the same bogus name to her pet Tamogotchi, which kept dying of starvation and neglect! Was that to be my eventual fate?

As a previous unknown, I was really surprised when the Wickford Pioneer Church trusted me with sharing at length about my vision, and my first week on the road. Their after-church tea and doughnuts were also an inspiration.

> "We did so enjoy – no, 'enjoy' is the wrong word – we did so feel a part of what you were doing, as we read your daily blog. We felt challenged and elated in turn, as we saw what God was doing to you and through you. Your visit to our church in Wickford was also a wake-up call, and helped us to identify where we had settled for maintenance rather than mission. So we have continued in our efforts to 'turn the ship around' and start in a more fruitful direction. Thanks again for your input and challenges."
>
> *Malcolm, Joan and Rhianna*

On the way to Maldon I became a traffic hazard to unsuspecting pedestrians, who had to slalom around my torpid body. Yes, I really did snooze right off, totally blocking the country footpath. One minute I was munching my sandwiches, the next I was away with the fairies. Ever get that same after-lunch feeling? Some elderly couple felt it was their duty to give me a swift kick in the side: lucky they did, otherwise I could have been there for the rest of the afternoon, and into the evening.

How about Trevor and Susie's church in Maldon? Growth rate 0 to 115 in four years! Not bad, as churches are meant to be dying ... On the way to Colchester, I was amazed to find from checking my emails that the blog (my internet diary) had really taken off. People were reading it, and praying for me in such places as America, Australia, Brazil, Czechia, and France – to mention just a few. Later on in the walk, I was to enquire of Luke, the chief web technician back home, just how many hits the website was receiving per month. To my astonishment, he came back with the reply of "5,000 minimum!"

Not only that – I was also receiving letters from friends back home who were following my reports in some detail...

Date 18th April

"Hello, Gary! You are surely a man who lives a charmed existence! Fancy arriving at a house where they fix your feet. Glad you managed to get over the wood episode! Watch out, as some of the leaves are spiky. We are all praying for you this end, and are really encouraged by what we hear."

Tim

Harwich (Felixstowe), Woodbridge, Saxmundham, Lowestoft = 72 miles

It was at the home of my Harwich hosts that I first lost my phone. This close friend had become essential to the walk, not only for calls, but for emails, blogs, and the website. It had a sliding keyboard and everything. Its loss was important enough to mention to my new acquaintances and even to worry about. I sent up a prayer. To my embarrassment, it was found (not by me) resting on top of the loo and minding its own business. Fortunately, my hosts made it out of that toilet alive, considering it still carried an interesting fragrance from my earlier visit. A number of my friends are familiar with that scent, and could even possibly use it to track me down if necessary.

True – blisters, heavy rain and twenty miles plus did not make a good combo – but Nigel and his wife cheered me up. He was always joking. However, there was one life-moving moment that I will never forget, and which is still fresh in my mind as I write this account. All of a sudden Nigel turned serious, but didn't lose the sparkling glint in his eye, as he said: "Gary, I have one thing to tell you about this walk – blinking enjoy it, boy!"

Nigel, who is a big gun in Crusaders (now Urban Saints), walked the first part of the day with me, as we trekked towards Woodbridge, and we were joined by Norman (aka Normski), a friend from church. There was definitely a chance to battle with the elements together, but this only served to inspire our conversation. My companions had a lot to say to each other about bus ministry, in which Normski specializes; it turned out that Nigel had been thinking about it for a while. The whole thing ended up with them making a plan for a shared project. That is what I call a divine appointment.

Saxmundham was the next port of call, and my Wood-bridge host Barbara joined me for the first six miles that day. She had a shocking life story as a result of an abusive childhood. Her parents saw her as a "waste of space", and did not even allow her on family holidays, because she would "get in the way". She was regularly bullied, verbally and physically. Then one day she was at the cinema, idly minding her own business, when the God she never knew swooped down into her life and gave her an identity she never had before. Barb's husband Bill took over the walking baton from her for the last part of that day. The fish and chips we ate together at Sweffling were worth remembering. A nice, bone-free piece of cod smothered in greasy, dripping batter along with those chunky chips that everyone loves. So, thanks to Bill, I had another superb sample of Suffolk cuisine before he tickled my spiritual taste-buds with these words: "I will always remember this; the experience has been one of the treasures of my life."

"We were delighted to have Gary stay with us in Wood-bridge. We understood that all he asked for was to be able to have shelter, even if it was the shed! This showed the heart of a humble servant. Both of us took turns in walking with him – it was one of those days of continuous rain, but it was still good. We valued the fact that Gary was a strong young man, and that he belonged to a church who saw the potential, and gave support. All of us who helped in some small measure must have believed that God would do more for Gary than he would expect, or dream of!"

Bill and Barbara

It is a good job that I think that people are more important than places, or that week's never-ending rain might have persuaded me to make an extended stopover sheltering with my Saxmundham hosts – some palace! The food was tasty too. It is not every day that my taste buds are tickled by salmon and cucumber quaffs – scrumptious. I must have a French streak in me, because I loved sitting down and simply talking about anything and everything for hours at the meal table with Richard and Viv, together with their family. That type of relational life suits me down to the ground!

So much happened in Lowestoft that it also features in a couple of chapters elsewhere. It was here that I stayed with one of my many favourite families. They were quite clear about the fact that they weren't Christians, but I felt so at home with them. I knew from the start that they were really interested in me, and discovered that they were quite surprised to find I was "normal". All our conversations were refreshing, and very honest. I was delighted that Malcolm, Liz and James kept in touch with me for months afterwards.

Horstead, Lyng, Fakenham, King's Lynn = 87 miles

A whole week of walking companions from my home church was to follow, set up by Vincent. On the way to Horstead, my mate Tim Burgess (the expert bridge builder) and I climbed countless steps in order to have a tower-top prayer and worship session, overlooking a vast area of Norfolk. As our MP3 players competed with the singing of the birds, we were interrupted by two Quakers seeking stillness. Actually, we had a really good chat with them, and exchanged varying opinions about Jesus' personality and mission.

As the day drew to a close I found myself settling down at George and Marcella's. They were caretakers for Matthew Fleming's house. I'm sure I don't need to tell you that he was a famous Kent cricketer. Marcella's cake set a standard that future hosts would find hard to match. The Czechs certainly found the way to my heart via my belly.

Jerry Freeman, Dymchurch's one and only fanatical Derby City fan, just about made it that night to meet up with me, before the next day's walk began. Due to the effect of ageing both on his car and his navigational skills, it actually took him nine hours to do the comfortable three and a half hour trip from Hythe. But it certainly proved worthwhile when he finally arrived, as it was so relaxing to spend the day being ourselves with God and each other. Jerry came with such a good attitude towards the walk, and I felt under no pressure to try to perform spiritually for his benefit. With Jerry, what you see is what you get, and that somehow rubbed off on me in such a way that I could be myself, no holds barred. We spent an age in a pub sharing the good news with a couple of locals who felt it necessary to direct us towards the famous prayer shrine in Great Walsingham. Sorry, but we didn't make it!

That evening we arrived in Lyng, one of the many overnight locations of which I had never previously heard. You might wonder why we chose that particular rural hide-out. Not for the first time, I was to go somewhere for the very good reason that someone back home had a connection. Vincent's relatives Robin and Christine lived there. Their interest in the walk was obvious. This was another pattern that was to surprise me over the walk. People from all ages and backgrounds seemed to enter totally into the spirit of the project.

Next morning, Robin suggested a risk-taking short cut over a dismantled railway track, through a big wood. What he didn't know was that recent heavy rainfall had produced a kind of moat, that almost encircled us. But by the time Vincent (who was that day's companion) and I discovered this, we had gone so far that there was no way we were turning back. Although neither of us had graduated as Boy Scouts, we bodged a perilous bridge from a rotten tree trunk. This was Indiana Jones stuff. It was then a bit disconcerting to find that we were now trapped between the so-called bridge and a barbed wire fence. At this point, Vincent insists on a mention of the fact that whilst I, as a typical sample of today's under-thirties, got completely stuck trying to scale the fence, he scored for the over-fifties by getting to the other side in a flash via an impressive commando-roll. Before we knew it, we were in Fakenham.

Two days in a row for the V man caused him to rise slightly slower than usual from our pub lunch. We went for something that was to become our custom, although totally out of keeping with anything that we had previously done in Kent. We entered an unlocked village church in Castle Rising, and for some inexplicable reason we found ourselves standing at the piano belting out some Christian numbers, old and new alike. The fires of Vincent's once mellow voice have somewhat faded with time, although he managed to at least dilute my lifelong tendency to wander tonelessly and with gusto from one key to another. So it was a bit of a shock when an old lady suddenly appeared round the corner, and said how much she had enjoyed listening to us. Disappointingly, perhaps, the ensuing conversation somewhat quickly demonstrated that she was actually fairly hard of hearing! As we dragged our weary limbs up the road to James and Anniece's abode in King's Lynn, we saw Roger swaggering out of his car, fresh and ready to go at once.

I soon retired to my bedroom, shattered from the day's walk, but with the words Squibbs had sent a couple of weeks earlier still in the back of my mind.

"Lord, walk with me.
Help me, as I put one foot in front of the other.
Direct my steps.
Be Thou my cover.

Lord, walk with me.
Unclutter my mind, to meditate on Your word,
So that I may know
You are the Lord.

Lord, walk with me.
Guide Thou my steps.
Lead me to where You want me to be,
Telling others of Your love,
How You can set them free.

Lord, walk with me.
I don't want to walk alone.
Be there at my side,
My constant Friend and Guide."

Holbeach, Boston, Friskney, Skegness = 62 miles

Roger and I woke to find that the cooked breakfast awaiting us was quite something – what you might call the whole shebang. White pudding, black pudding, home made hash browns; you name it, we got it. Most importantly, James and Anniece sent us off with much prayer.

Roger had his first taste of praying aloud on the streets with a random bloke who called us over from the other side of the road to talk about his garden. Alan Titchmarsh II? He really opened up as we talked about the purpose of our journey, and was only too keen to tell us about his forthcoming neck operation. We left him with the opportunity to read for himself about how he could get to know God, and travelled on towards Holbeach.

My next host, Kevin, had arranged a press interview with a couple of different local papers, who were to produce very encouraging reports. As we hopped into the car to go to the half-night prayer meeting, my friend Jim phoned to say that he was recommitting his life to God, after ten years of being away. It must have looked quite strange to Kevin, as I struggled to contain my excitement within the confines of his car.

Now to keep another promise – a mention of one of Kevin's little character oddities. How many other people do you know who truly relish an appetizing cocktail of ice cream and jelly babies? Presumably that extravagant sugar injection fuels him up each Friday for the late night prayer marathon? No doubt it was because I declined the offer of a personal supply of that unique concoction that I found myself continuously and uncontrollably nodding off. Good job one shuts one's eyes to pray, or I would have had to resort to that well-known cover-up phrase – "I'm merely resting my eyes!" Hmmm . . .

Mum, my brothers Tony and Mark, and friend Shane joined me really early for some breakfast, before we hit the road to Boston. They did a relay approach. Mum walked the first leg, while the lads were in the car, and then swapped over. The whole plan – sneakily organized by my Notting-ham Forest mad brother – was to have this day's walk polished off before lunch time. Mark's aim was to enable us to enjoy the questionable pleasure of watching Forest play – if that's what you call it! They did win, and lived to fight another battle or two in their doomed attempt to avoid relegation. My day also included sponsoring a girl who was running a marathon to raise money for cancer victims. I kept quiet about the fact that I was on a shoestring budget myself, and was really thinking she could have equally considered helping me out.

Stuart and Karen's welcome was amazingly warm towards all five of us, and I had a great opportunity to share at their Boston church. Then my family left, and my hosts took me out to lunch, where I whipped down a pizza. I spent the afternoon at my uncle and aunt's, who have a lovely house on the river near by. I hadn't seen them since I was about five. My nan and grandad were staying with them.

Stuart was the youngest pastor I met on my travels, a mere couple of years older than myself. He was full of adventure and lively ideas. We had something else in common – ever-empty bellies and our love for a late evening bit of nosh in the form of a juicy kebab. I was to regret it the next morning!

My extended weekend in Boston also included my first morning lie-in for ages. A friend from back home, John Rawlings, had taught me how to fix my GPS when it stalled.

I put my lesson to good practice. Isn't it like God to have given me a couple of free hours to do so for the first time?

Next stop was Friskney, with several more new companions. Maybe I should mention another record? Karen's little girl can't have been more than a year old, but she came as a kind of conscript, as mum brought her along in her buggy. After about a mile, they reassigned themselves to less arduous duties, but their friend Dave pushed on the whole way to Friskney. Norman – although a great host in so many ways – sadly missed a trick, by failing to have Sky Sports even though he had a Sky digibox. Liverpool were on, but I ended up watching a blank screen, and using the radio commentary to feed my imagination. Norman made up for it, though, with his incredible piano playing. Elton John, eat your heart out.

Plodding on, I found that still more people gladly joined me. Phil and I exchanged life stories as we walked. He had been involved with similar Christian youth work, and I found him easy to talk to. Rachel, his girlfriend, joined us on her bike, but she couldn't make it all the way, as it decided to rain. We had to trek across some rather uneven ploughed fields, spiked with clods of drying mud. My boots took a bit of a battering, and by the time we reached Skegness the soles had doubled in size and weight with sticky goo picked up as we squelched along. En route, what I would call a weird happening came our way, as we chatted to someone doing a bit of labour in their garden. The guy was an atheist who wanted to disprove Christianity. As he walked away angrily from the conversation I noticed a serious limp, so I shouted across to him offering prayer. A bold and crazy step? Yes, I know! He turned, telling us about this dodgy hip and how he would love some prayer, even though just moments earlier he had been giving us the third degree. Of course we obliged, and it was a lovely moment. I felt gutted that God didn't choose to heal him there and then, though. But who knows?

Sutton on Sea, North Somercotes, Grimsby, Brigg = 65 miles

Sutton on Sea saw three friends from home take a trip in the car to see me. Church big-boss-man Graham and his wife Deirdre came to walk with me. Their chauffeur was Mike Hands, our friendly local funeral director. No, I hadn't decided to end the walk prematurely! Like my family a few days earlier, the three of them did the walk in a relay fashion. It was so nice to see friends. It takes a while to forge a decent relationship, and I was sadly aware that many of the contacts I had made along the way would be fleeting friendships. My hosts Paul and Michelle go down as having the hottest bathroom in existence. It was kind of like a sauna. To get the desired effect, all you have to do is put up with a little bit of noise. Ingredients: tumble-dryer and washing machine going full pelt.

That night we had a great prayer meeting! Some random Joe Bloggs prophesied that God would really use me, and give me the nation. Hmmm . . . I was up for it, but doubt plagued my cynical mind.

Onwards and upwards, off towards the summer-coats of the north. To all young people, I'm so sorry, because that day I officially became old. Slowly and scarily I have started to enjoy the more simple things of life like just watching birds fly, and listening to them make music, admiring beautiful scenery, and taking an interest in watching an ant carry a load across the street. Yes, before long I will probably be watching trains and collecting stamps.

I have no idea what birds I saw, but they were stunning. Marie, that night's host, proved to be very hospitable. She had one of the more challenging jobs, dealing with and counselling people who had suffered abuse. It didn't surprise me that Marie had found that God really helped her with her work, and she had some amazing answers to prayer.

James and Grimsby! Now then, what can I say? This deserves a chapter all of its own. James and Louise have been friends for quite a while, even though they are from further north than my beloved Folkestone – but for now let's talk about his uncle and aunty who put me up for the night. Although Susan and her husband were not followers of the Way, they treated me like royalty, providing me with some wonderful hospitality. They made me feel like I was the centre of their attention. We had a roast that Gordon Ramsay would have been proud of, and the supply of beer was free flowing. We ended up having a bowl of peanuts, whilst watching the snooker World Championship.

Twenty one miles from Grimsby to Brigg in the blazing heat was a challenge. In a pub in the sticks, I came across a couple whom I'd met at church in Grimsby a day earlier. They left me with a kind gift, which was to pay for scrumptious pub lunches over the next few days. Ironically, having started the day in shorts and tee-shirt, I ended it wrapped up in a winter coat as the heavens opened on my hosts' pre-arranged garden barbecue, to which they had invited many friends and neighbours. The downpour didn't last too long, though, and I was able to kick a ball about with the children there. Not bad, eh, after an unusually long stretch! It was hard to relax in the evening as my first soldier host, Keith, told me some horror stories of what one human being can do to another – and all because of hate.

I got out a letter from home that I had recently received to switch my mind off.

"Hi Gary,
We are unable to follow your progress daily on the website due to our computer not working. But we did enjoy reading your latest newsletter. Pete had a cold water baptism when someone forget to check if the heating was on in the pool – like you, he knows what it is like to have cold bath. How are

the dreaded blisters? I've heard that two pairs of socks is what is needed. I usually pray for you whilst delivering the papers around 7 a.m. daily. I even had a dream, but it did not make sense. In my dream we met up, and joined you in a city. At first I thought it was London, but as you didn't go there it can't have been. Then I saw you further on in what I assume was Yorkshire. My friend who lives in Cumbria was also there but we were about to head off along what I believe was the Cleveland Way, where I had done some walking before. (Be careful, Gary, the Cleveland Way is partly a cliff top.) Then I woke up, and – if nothing else – my dream had prompted me to pray. I don't know what else the dream was trying to say. I would love to join you at some point but this would need prayer, and lots of it. My friend Maggie told me you should appeal to local radio stations for walking companions. She has also heard that the bishop of Cumbria and a friend are thinking of walking around the county, and she thinks that they would gladly join you. As I write this, I am conscious of the 'Footprints in the Sand' poem. I am specially thinking of the part where it says about the Lord carrying us in the tough times. Gary, the Lord is going to carry you on the tough days ahead, and He is with you all the way. Stay safe."

Tina, Peter, Dianne and Shane

Hull, Driffield, Scarborough, Whitby = 92 miles

In order to reach Amy and Ryan's home in Hull, I needed to tackle the Humber Bridge. It was plain massive, and a bit intimidating. The wind decided to play a role as I tried to take some snaps. I wonder if other people ever experience the same insane momentary urge to jump off, and say goodbye to this world? I consider myself to be a lover of life, so when the voice whispered in my ear it was rejected quickly, knowing that it was no part of the real me. Baby Thomas was lovely, but kept looking very curiously at this new found stranger in his home. He and his parents were about to go off for the weekend as I arrived. Although we had known each other for a mere hour, they left me with their key and free rein of TV and fridge overnight. What trust, and what an opportunity to relish the sight of Liverpool knocking Chelsea out of the Champions' League, whilst indulging in my strawberries and cream! The only stress of the whole occasion was the worry of having to wake myself from my hoggish slumbers, without the usual aid of a merciful host to knock on the door with a wake-up call.

I found out on my travels towards Driffield that it is actually possible to read and walk simultaneously for a long period of time without twisting an ankle. But don't try this at home, folks! I was inspired again to reflect on God's love toward mankind, as expressed in His unconditional gift of freewill. It reminded me of a famous quote from the film *Braveheart*, which my friends and I frequently and no doubt annoyingly spout. "Your heart is free, William. Have the courage to follow it." I believe that when we receive God's grace our hearts become alive, so we can dare to follow them.

As the day drew to a close, I spent an hour chatting about everything under the sun to a guy from the land of the white cliffs, whilst we sipped tea at his table. I stayed up late in Steve and Angela's home, where the night's entertainment included a game of Cluedo. Victory was mine for the taking, but I committed an error and made myself look like a donkey instead. I retreated soon afterwards up the many flights of stairs which led to my attic room, with the unfortunate result that every time I needed something from downstairs I had to complete what seemed like another day's walk in order to collect it.

Whilst just 37% of the British population was obeying Tony Blair's call to go to the polls, I was strolling towards

Bridlington ignoring his summons. I received my due punish-
ment. A homing seagull sent from 10 Downing Street was
directly on target, leaving me with a crown of splendour. As
Bob treated me to a takeaway, I reflected once again on the
distinct possibility of becoming the first person to walk around
Britain and return with a massive gut. I was disappointed with
myself, as again I found it hard to build a meaningful
connection with someone who had been kind enough to put
me up for the night. It dawned on me that – even with my
incredibly charming personality – it would not be possible to
hit it off with everyone I met along the way.

It is absolutely amazing that every day I was in the care of
new hosts, most of whom I didn't know before, but who were
at least in good health. So what can I say about Jim and Pat,
who stood by their commitment to put me up despite being
under the weather? Usually I was the one noticeably struggling to stay awake, but poor Jim literally kept falling asleep,
no matter how hard he tried not to. Pat has quite a story of
how she kept knocking on God's door for Jim to come
through and be a friend of Jesus. Jim resisted for many years
by filling his life with football, martial arts and alcohol, but
eventually one day, on bended knee and with many tears, he
opened up his damaged heart to God. He had hurt many of his
family by his licentious life style. God immediately planted in
his heart a desire to seek forgiveness from them.

As I left Scarborough, its famous 800-year-old castle grew
fainter and fainter through the haze, but the bright coastline
quickly became exciting. Several headlands stood out, which
would need to be conquered on the way to Robin Hood's
Bay. It was painfully obvious that several very steep ups-and-
downs were to be an early challenge for my legs that day.

Coming towards Robin Hood's Bay, you can see signs of
sea erosion, which the locals reckon is happening at a rate
of five centimetres every year, only partly slowed up by the
sea wall built in 1975. It would have been exciting to live here

two hundred and fifty years ago, when smuggling was at its height, and rum, brandy and tobacco were secretly and silently passed along a maze of passages and tunnels and into safe hiding from the king's officers. Now that would have been an adventure! Close by this picturesque village is Boggle Hole, where smugglers used to land their contraband, and which tradition tells us is inhabited by boggles, or hobgoblins, the "little people" who were thought to live in caves along the coast, as well as in the more remote parts of the nearby Yorkshire Moors. But I didn't meet any!

The magnificent and slightly threatening remains of Whitby Abbey tower into view for miles in advance. Having been more than once to Bran Castle in Romania, known to the locals as Dracula's Castle, my interest was captured by the discovery that Whitby is reckoned to be Bram Stoker's inspiration for the story. By the time I reached the town, my feet were speaking quite loudly. No doubt if there had been only one hundred and ninety eight steps needed to climb up to St Mary's church next to the Abbey I would have given it a go; it was finding there was that extra one which produced a hesitation, and instead led my feet to trek straight for my hosts' home, without stopping to ask for my permission.

My phone had been out of signal for a number of days. It felt slightly odd knowing that friends and family had not been able to follow my daily progress via blog. So it was good to finally catch up, and be in touch again. Once again it made me realize that my phone was pivotal to the adventure as planned. I latched on to the Cleveland Way, which I was to follow for a number of days. The views were spectacular, and the best I had seen thus far on my journey. I remember it for the high cliffs and the deep blue of the North Sea.

Sheenagh and Prasanna let me have their luxurious holiday flat for the weekend break. It was fully equipped with a stuffed fridge and spa bath which I took full advantage of. My tired muscles wallowed in hot bubbling water, and the world seemed a beautiful place to live in. Prasanna had some interesting theories relating to mental illness, and the effect of too much sugar on the brain. This subject is close to my heart and I found myself trying to apply his ideas to a situation in my own family. I spoke at Whitby church that morning. I was beginning to get a flavour of so many churches, In Whitby it felt like I belonged, which was great!

Loftus, Redcar, Teeside, Hartlepool = 49 miles

Not having reached Scotland yet, I mistook the Loftus hills for mountains. It is not often that you pop into a pub and a guy greets you with the fact that he wants to die. When I told him about God wanting to help, he said that his God was whisky. He mocked the *Knowing God* book that I offered him. With my heart in my mouth, I stood up and stretched over to place it in his blazer pocket. Instead of smacking me in the face, he simply grabbed my hand and held on to it, with a look of desperation on his face.

In the same pub was another fella fighting a different kind of battle. He had cancer of the throat, and the doctors had given him only two months to live. I prayed for him.

I stayed one night in a foster home. Dave previously lived and breathed cars along with a girlfriend who he thought he loved. He first became aware of God's love through his car tuner friend. This man's lifestyle was so different that one day Dave turned up unannounced for a cuppa, and was promptly invited to church. He almost gave up at once, because nobody really welcomed him. Thankfully, at the critical moment one man approached him, and from there on everything changed.

However hard I tried, I couldn't find anyone in the village of Redcar that Noreen didn't know! Although she is obviously in her seventies, her house is the centre of continual comings and goings. She produced a lush dinner with a home-made fruit salad, one sure way to my heart. Her past is full of difficult incidents, but God has given her the gift of joy. She spends all her time concentrating on "being" rather than "doing". Happy people are contagious, and she was!

> "Gary was a joy to have staying in my home in Redcar – such a charming young man, so well mannered, and definitely focused on his prayer walk. It made me wish I was still young and healthy so I could have walked with him for part of his journey. I followed his blog for several months, although my PC crashed after a while. Just after I got it going again, I heard the good news that he was due home having completed the walk. I always knew Gary would be safe, as God was with him all the way on his walk. It was plain to see how much he loved God in every word he spoke, and I know that God loves him.
>
> As Gary would say – 'Chow!' "
>
> *Noreen*

There was next to no-one about as I crossed farms and trudged along narrow footpaths. One farmer said I was the first person to walk his footpath that year – not surprising, as I couldn't even see where it was! It was great to catch up and stay with friends. John and I watched *Dumb and Dumber* together, and ended up bent over in stitches. It has to be my all-time favourite movie. I got to thinking again what tremendous freedom there is in a good laugh. A merry heart does act as a medicine, according to Proverbs 17:22. As I pushed off to bed, John's mum did what all good mums do, and reminded me very nicely to make sure everything was packed in the morning and especially not to forget anything. Guess what I did?

So much for my satellite navigation system, John and I had to choose from four footpath options, none of which existed on my map. We eventually located and crossed the bridge we wanted, but on the other side the path turned in to a manky swamp. We had two options – to go back, or climb the steep bank ahead of us. We made what turned out to be the wrong choice, ending up in the middle of Tees-side steelworks. We had unknowingly avoided all the protective fences, and had been walking along their private road for several miles. The angry shouts of a foreman soon made us aware of our unpopular blunder. We were seen off by way of the nearest fence. I am still not so sure that the foreman believed me when I told him that our meeting was no accident, and that God loved him. Remarkably, we were no sooner over the fence than we got lost again. When we finally picked up the right path we encountered a couple of train spotters and had a good chat, sowing seeds of the gospel. At lunchtime we met up with Tom, one of my house-mates back home, and after tucking in unreservedly, we began the long drive back to Kent for my first home break.

Hartlepool 16th May – Helmsdale 25th June

Sunderland, Tynemouth, Ashington, Alnwick, Holy Island = 104 miles

I must admit I was a bit worried about getting the times right on the Island causeway, since I didn't want to disappear with the incoming tide. But I was not expecting to have my problem solved by three beauts who drove alongside at the critical moment and temporarily abducted me. Not that I resisted, you understand! They seconded me to lead them on an educational tour of the Island, which I of course managed to extend into the early afternoon. But even their charms faded in the anticipation of the up and coming FA Cup Final. Aaaagh, but where to watch it? Wasn't I due to be staying at a monastery where the monks would be more into prayer than footie?

It seemed that my worst fears were confirmed, as my hosts showed me around their monk house. No matter how hard I looked, not a trace of a TV wire was to be seen. But desperation drives us to bizarre extremes! How rude of me, after less than five minutes' acquaintance, to dare to ask if there was any chance of me watching the Cup Final somewhere. Then the impossible happened. Brother Damien rolled back the sofa to reveal its hidden secret. There, on a puny table, perched all alone and covered in dust, stood my ageing life saver! Would you believe it was in colour as well?

As a Christian I was expecting a spiritual experience of some kind, and I was not disappointed. My monk friends were not only dedicated, but so humble in the way that they sought the opinion of someone less than half their age concerning topics on which they could have considered themselves experts. I felt honoured as they served me a double helping of their meagre portions. Their lifestyle made such an impact on me that, apparently from nowhere, came the thought of wanting to take away something of what they had, and I didn't have a clue what it was . . . although I know what it wasn't! But it gave me food for thought, as I crossed the Scottish border.

"We enjoyed Gary's visit to Holy Island very much. Although he left in the rain. I hope he was also blessed by the occasion, and by this place, which draws so much goodness out of people. The peace of the Lord be always with you!"
Signed by Brother Damien (provincial bursar)

Berwick-upon-Tweed, Eyemouth, North Berwick = 58 miles

Some Czech friends who made it their habit to visit sick people emailed me Cyril's address in Eyemouth, so I made contact. Like many others in his critical condition, Cyril seemed to be blaming God, rather than looking to Him for help. I knew that I was there to comfort rather than to argue with him. Later, Eric and Edna pooled their experiences of Africa with mine. They outdid me because at that time I was still safari-less, though I have since put that right. Like a donkey, I forgot my camera when Eric took me out on his yacht, which was a pity since the views from St Abbe's Head were breathtaking. It is also a shame that I can't remember too much of Eric's impromptu lesson on Scottish sea birds! What was it again . . . Lesser Spotted Puffi-Gullock?

Uncanny, don't you think, that just one day later I was to sit watching a programme concerning monasteries, one that went down very well with the British public? In this age of reality TV shows it could seem hard to find a different approach, but this one succeeded. Everyday Joes were exposed to the radical lifestyle of a solemn monastery over a period of time. My own recent experience meant I was not surprised that they were challenged and changed. One guy, you may recall, even gave up his job in the soft porn industry as a result of watching!

My walk to North Berwick got under way unusually early, as I planned to spend a bit more time there before reaching Bill and Sally's home. I had felt challenged the day earlier to give people my ears, yeah – the both of 'em! Enough to crush a man! I spent most of the afternoon sitting on the same bench in glorious sunshine, as one person after another came and sat telling me their life stories.

Bill lost no time in majorly bigging up the panoramic sea views from his balcony. My new found enthusiasm for scenery took me up there like a shot – bit of a nightmare for us both to find the spectacle ruined by an artistic creation in wood and metal superimposed by some philistine scaffolding friends. Later, Bill temporarily re-awakened my dormant desire to become the next Jimmy Hendrix as he skillfully plucked his Fender Stratocaster (not that I'm jealous) through the sultry moonlit evening.

Nunraw Abbey, Musselburgh, Edinburgh, Cowdenbeath, Kirkcaldy = 72 miles

As I left behind yet another monkery challenge and headed for Musselburgh I could still hear "You'll Never Walk Alone" ringing in my ears, following Liverpool's heroic victory over AC Milan the previous night. Steve's church was packed to the seams and more, as a dedication service took place. Many non-Christians were there for the first time, which meant sharing about the walk took on an extra edge. I spent some precious time cutting and pasting with a great guy who also happened to be autistic. I was on cutting and gluing and he was on pasting, and frankly I couldn't keep up with his mind-blowing speed.

Edinburgh is a great city, and clearly a must, being the Scottish capital and home of the world famous Princes Street. All around me were examples of ancient architecture which the likes of my friend Sam would have enjoyed, though maybe even he would take a while to get through all the city's "listed" buildings – over four thousand of them. To have planned to walk through Edinburgh two months later would have been sensible, if I had wanted to be part of the world-famous annual Festival, one of many major attractions somehow drawing over thirteen million visitors to the city each year. Not bad for a city whose local population is still under half a million.

With its unique blend of hills and valleys, the sea close by, and so many amazing places of interest, I could see why many people describe the place as dramatic. But the castle, perched high above the city, dominates everything. Each of its one million visitors every year not only gets a big dose of Scottish history but also incredible panoramic views of the locality. That is, of course, if their hearts survive the shock of hearing the "one o'clock gun", which certainly captures the unwary visitor's attention! Close by is the Witches' Well, the site where many women were burnt at the stake on suspicion of being witches. It scares me to think how many of them would have been totally innocent, and how they must have felt after hearing themselves condemned.

I can remember as if it were yesterday going down to the pier with Eva, a Czech friend, and facing the wind as we walked along. It seemed to go on for miles, and I was petrified. It was so windy, I honestly felt like I was going to fall into the sea.

Tibbermore, Dundee, Arbroath, Montrose = 97 miles

On the way to Montrose, I met a couple of drunks sitting on a bench with their withered looking dogs and a bottle of whisky in an old brown bag. It seemed best to opt for walking on like the priest and the Levite, but God gave me a Good Samaritan moment and I felt that I couldn't simply pass by. As is so often the case, everything was just fine, and God really helped me to share His message of hope with them. The drunks were on the edge of their bench as they listened intently.

No sooner was one fear conquered than another surfaced. This time it was a group of youths shouting abuse at an old guy on a bike as he passed them playing football. Seconds later they turned their attention to me, but I couldn't pick up their accents. However, football is an international language and I asked to play. They agreed, and heads and volleys began. What on earth was I doing, joining in after having already walked fifteen miles? I wasn't exactly dressed for the beautiful game, and they all found it pretty hilarious watching me try to kick the ball in my hiking boots. To make things worse, the heavens suddenly opened, and the kick-around soon became a mudbath. Despite getting soaked, I was able to share my journey with them as we played on for at least another hour.

By the time I reached Montrose for a long weekend, the realization hit me that I was well and truly into the third month of the walk. Clive, Hazel and their son Derek dried me off, and took care of me. Church was great, golf was victorious (sorry, Derek), food was top-drawer. Derek and I dropped in on the local press who agreed to feature the walk in their next publication, but I hadn't expected such a long and glowing report to appear in the *Montrose Review*, apparently one of the oldest newspapers in Scotland!

> "We had a very good long weekend with Gary and the timing was really excellent, because our son who is in his twenties was here for the weekend. Our local paper took interest in his visit, and printed a covering article the following week."
>
> *Clive Alder*

Inverbervie, Muchalls, Aberdeen = 39 miles

Out of all the churches I had the opportunity to be a part of, Inverbervie is close to being my favourite. There was so much enthusiasm for God in the midweek meeting I attended. It set me free to be myself right from the outset. It's hard to explain, but even as I first walked into the village I felt the presence of God in an almost tangible way. As soon as I arrived at my hosts I was offered a beer, and it was then I felt I must have reached heaven on earth.

I met Dot back at Inverbervie. A couple of days later, early in the morning, she was driving near Muchalls, about twenty miles from her home, when she suddenly felt moved in her heart to pray for me. It was clearly a God-incident, since moments later she actually passed me on the road, and pulled over to share what had happened. As you can imagine, we then spent a few precious moments praying together, both relishing the knowledge that God can direct the theme and the timing of our prayers.

As I reached the coast heading for Aberdeen, it was still so early that the beaches were empty of people, and the sheer beauty of God's creation once again hit me between the eyes. In true caveman style, I decided to fashion a writing implement from a piece of driftwood, using my Swiss army knife. Well, I felt I had to use it, since it was bought! Some favourite Psalms are actually etched on my memory, and I wanted to inscribe the words into the pristine sands as a testimony to those who would later follow me onto the beach. It was in my heart to let everybody know who had created it all.

There was another good moment when I realized that God, not Gary, was sourcing the idea in my mind to purchase a camcorder, to use not only for recording the beauties of His world, and documenting random street interviews, but also for giving hosts the opportunity to air their opinions. It felt like there was no time to lose and the video camera got its first outing, as its price tag certainly demanded that it be used without delay. I decided that – as this adventure was to do with prayer – there could be no better place to start than with an interview about it.

> [*Question*]: What does prayer mean to you as an individual?
> [*Sandy*]: Prayer for me is communicating with God.
> [*Jane*]: It is God talking back so I can hear what He wants to say to me. I just tell Him whatever I am feeling or wanting.
> [*Sandy*]: Every night, we have a focused time of prayer and commit our day back to God. That way, life is a continual conversation with God.

Being with Jay reminded me about my brother back home, who also suffers from hearing "voices". She had the same challenging (and slightly refreshing) quality common to the condition – of speaking out exactly what was going on in her mind, rather than dressing up a rude remark to sound acceptable. As a family, we have had to learn to accept people with diverse personalities.

Next morning – to my sheer delight – I found that a letter had been posted along with some other regular weekly supplies including my week's itinerary, stamps, website cards, tracts, gift vouchers, and the like.

> "Greetings from Hythe. Hope you are well and your feet are bearing up. We are praying for you each day – divine appointments, good rapport with hosts, words of knowledge and wisdom, and that you would see miracles. On Saturday we took Tim to London for an early Father's Day outing. Father's Day is actually Sunday 19th June, just in case you needed a reminder! We went to Hyde Park for lunch, and saw the Princess Diana memorial fountain. I can't help thinking she would have preferred the money to go to AIDS victims in Africa. Tim is well, and is growing a pair of fairly short side burns. They look very handsome. He sends his love, but had to leave for work before the letter writing began. Believe for miracles."
>
> **Ness**

Inverurie, Newburgh, Peterhead = 51 miles

Inverurie, I bet you'd never heard of that town until you saw it on this page! Well, it may come as a surprise to you, but it has a bit of a lengthy history which stretches back a tad further than even the memorable battle of Hastings. But its big moment came just under six hundred years ago, at nearby Harlaw, when apparently it was the scene of one of the most savage battles ever fought on soggy Scottish soil.

My own struggle was not with armed soldiers but with the forces of nature. No doubt there are some periods when it doesn't rain on the road from Newburgh to Peterhead, but I definitely didn't have the joy of experiencing one.

In Peterhead, where Elizabeth hosted me overnight, I was really impressed by the local church youth group, and how they reached out to God.

Out came the video camera again and this time Charlie (father of my host, Elizabeth) was my willing victim . . .

[*Question*]: What is the real point of prayer?
[*Charlie*]: Prayer is a necessity, and it is always answered. Pray without ceasing in every circumstance. I have been through two major operations, removing first a tumour, then a kidney. Of course I was fearful, but people were praying, and I experienced total inner peace. Prayer addresses every situation, and the one thing that can stop me from praying is the enemy. He has this ability to use my weaknesses that he knows all too well. But through prayer God is working on those!

Fraserburgh, Banff, Cullen, Elgin, Nairn = 101 miles

According to the locals, Fraserburgh was once an internationally significant port. It started life as a town in 1546, and the famous harbour was already being used before the first stone pier was built here in 1576 by Sir Alexander Fraser, after whom it is named. Don't stop to be impressed by my knowledge just yet – there's more! Over three hundred years later, eight hundred fishing boats were based in Fraserburgh – almost one for every ten people living here at the time. Since that time, boats have become fewer, but their size has increased. In fact, some of the largest in any Scottish fishing port decorate the harbour of this grey stone town, which spins around the 1736 Mercat Cross. Apparently, any Scottish town or city whose life is dominated by trade still has a mercat, or market cross, but this is the only one which has both the royal arms of Scotland before it was joined to England, *and* the arms of the new United Kingdom under James I, whoever he was! The town castle was built in 1570, and a lighthouse erected on top of it 216 years later. Give me a hundred years, and I'll be a historian yet!

It was near Fraserburgh that I met John, who was part of a 2003 church plant in a small local village. Once again the video camera took over.

> [*Question*]: What stops you from praying, and what is your most amazing answer to prayer?
> [*John*]: The demands of my lifestyle are mostly what stop me from praying enough. What can be more amazing than to have seen God bring my daughter out of the depths of drug addiction, into the freedom of Jesus and all He has to offer?

That will do for the video camera interviews, otherwise we shall use up too many trees!

It's only since the walk began that I've become aware of things like the fact that Scotland and Ireland have their own variations of the Gaelic language. It turned out that Banff is an old Scottish poetic word for Ireland. On reaching the town, it was amazing to think that – after just seventy-six days – I was actually well over forty miles north of Aberdeen, and foraging ever deeper into places whose very names had been unknown to me until the last few months. Yes, I know, there were many good laughs back in the church office at this stage about the depths of my ignorance about British geography.

I met John in Elgin, where David and Louise had kindly treated me to a cinema trip to watch *Batman Begins*. So as I moved off next day towards Nairn, it goes without saying for someone like me that I felt like one of God's super-heroes, who with His help could rescue the world. If only feelings could sometimes translate into reality!

Loads of people were out in their gardens on such a gorgeous day – yes, the rain had somehow forgotten that it was supposed to happen every single day in Scotland, and had quite unaccountably stopped. In the north, people have time to stop and chat, and I lost count of the number of conversations I struck up along the way. Contrary to popular perception, the Scots also seem to be characterized by generosity, and for the third day in a row I was treated to a free pub lunch. Let that be an encouragement to the English pubs, whose score in this department so far is nil.

The host church in Nairn was to be the smallest for the whole walk – a mere ten of us got together on the Sunday morning. But I loved it – there was such intimacy, and so much ongoing participation by everyone present.

Inverness, Dingwall, Tain, Brora, Helmsdale = 88 miles

I somehow sloshed my way – or I might as well call it swimming, really – from Inverness to Dingwall, It was sleeting so hard all I could do was duck for cover before those ice drops actually knocked me clean out. Seeing a converted garage, which was kind of open I rudely sought shelter uninvited. To my surprise, I'd entered a work shop. Before long, Joe from North Kessock was telling me all about the secret of Targe-making. Basically, these are the sort of shields you might see in *Braveheart*! They were amazing – such fine detail! The video camera came out, and I felt privileged to be interviewing a guy who had made these targes for famous people all over the world. Sean Connery was one of the main recipients, as he had a load bought for his birthday one year.

On reaching Helmsdale, I stopped off in the local pub and got chatting to the locals, most of whom were intrigued by the walk. Some went so far as to try to give me money. One young lad, who had replaced working with drinking for the morning, became quite aggressive. Although he was obviously a regular among his friends, the others all took my side, defending my right to be a Jesus freak if I wanted to, even if my English accent was irritating to him. Not long afterwards he actually squared up to me, but I ignored him, ate my lunch pretty sharpish, and left!

By this time I was more than ready for an extended home-break, despite having to first endure a sixteen-hour drive, which was made very pleasant by Tim and Emma, who came up from Inverness to collect me. Birthday celebrations at home awaited me, to be followed by a few days of crisping up in Spain with Tony, Mark, Mevl, Shane and Steve.

Helmsdale (Orkney day trip), Lybster, Wick, John O'Groats = 52 miles

The eventual re-start from Helmsdale was made so much easier because I was heading back with my dad for company. However, I did create a few problems for myself – it's not only goldfish which are restricted to a five-second memory span! Throughout the walk, my GPS was my ever-present friend and informant; not a day could pass without us spending time together! It was the one thing I dared not leave behind. So it will come as no surprise to anyone who knows me, that when dad and I got out of Vincent's car at Heathrow airport, ready to fly back to Inverness, I neglected to check the boot thoroughly. Consequently, I managed to leave my GPS soul-mate behind. The SKCC admin team and the Post Office rose to the occasion, and a joyful reunion took place an impressive two days later.

My dad was even more struck than myself by the gener-osity and friendliness of the Scots, as we stopped for extended conversations with a whole variety of people over a couple of days.

At 7.55 that morning we joined the coach heading from Inverness to John O'Groats. There was an annoyingly long queue at the port, but we were really excited about the up and coming day-trip to Orkney, which would include a ferry crossing. From a distance, the islands looked surprisingly flat to a southern visitor who had recently been introduced for the first time to the breathtaking mountains of northern Scotland. I was surprised to see so many islets. Rugged cliffs, speckled with red, white, yellow, green and brown welcomed us, their faces weathered from centuries of exposure to the cruel attentions of the bleak Pentland Firth. Ah that's more like it!

As we neared our destination, the cliff faces showed themselves for what they were – stark and steep in true Scottish style. We were greeted by the sight of grazing grizzly bears, or were they Highland cattle in need of a serious haircut? As we moored up, Orkney looked a little lonely, although crowded with coaches. Towards Kirkwall things began to liven up. The place was full of very nice buildings, with an old sort of feel to them. We visited Skara Brae (Sandswick's Bay o'Skaill) and found ourselves nosily peering through someone's roof windows. I know what you are thinking, and – no – it definitely wasn't a case of a couple of voyeurs ogling some prehistoric cave girl. Instead it was just some Neolithic dry-stone houses seen from above. But even I could understand why this site is famous for being one of the most amazing monuments in the whole of Europe.

Of course, I had never heard before of the tremendous storm in 1850, when extreme gales and tides exposed the outline of a series of ancient buildings concealed in a large mound. I'm not great with museums, but this insight into lifestyle so long ago fascinated me. As I looked through the glass panel above the homes, each appeared to have something in common. There was a large, square room in which the fireplace was the focal point. Facing the entrance was some kind of shell dresser, and a stone bed stood on either side. How about that for a comfy night's kip?

The day was unusual because we were not walking a specific planned section from place to place. I was used to having time to take in all my surroundings as I wandered on foot, but now I was travelling ten times as quickly, and everything seemed to flash by remarkably fast. As my former schoolteachers could tell you, I'm not a huge fan of guided tours, but the guy in charge this time was actually very funny and kept us all from being bored. Dad also commented positively on his humour, and – to my surprise – loved the whole tour. I had been led to believe that there would be stack loads of puffins all over the place, but the only one we saw was the tour guide, as he threw his whole being into entertaining us.

We passed Scapa Flow on the way, and I must try to remember that this important harbour was discovered by King Haokon for his Viking fleet in the thirteenth century. Eight hundred years later it was a crucial base for British shipping in both World Wars. Not surprisingly, wreck-diving is a popular tourist attraction today for people who would like to see several of the major World War I warships and destroyers which still nestle on the seabed beneath the waves. I thought highly of this option, so long as it was for someone else! Would I have chickened out even if time had allowed?

Stromness is yet another northern settlement which to my untutored eyes looked perilously close to the edge of the landscape. The second largest town in the Orkney Islands, this ancient seaport lies on the southwest coast of the main island, but has a population of less than 2,500. We walked through the old town, which basically consists of one main street, with many narrow alleys forking from it – and at the end of each lies yet another magnificent sea-view. Stromness became politically prominent for a short while during the late seventeenth century, when England was at war with France, and shipping in general was forbidden to use the English Channel.

The Standing Stones were part of a mystical stone circle also known as the Ring of Brodgar, yet another Neolithic construction. Some people think it looks a bit like Stonehenge. It stands on a narrow strip of land, and is thought to be about 4,500 years old. I got out my long-distance steel rule and discovered that the diameter was 104 metres. With the aid of my calculator I counted the prints of some sixty stones, but found that only twenty-seven were still standing. People obviously care about this site, if the mown grass and attractive surrounding heather are anything to go by. Four of the stones towered above, casting threatening dark shadows like those of a giant tombstone. Had one fallen on top of me, it's definite that no further burial ceremony would have been necessary. Occasionally a stone lay flat in the circle, bearing an uncanny resemblance to the shadow of its erect comrades. I saw a visiting cyclist looking up at one of the stones; he looked like a pygmy in comparison.

What I am told is the red sandstone of St Magnus' cathedral dominates Kirkwall. Dad and I took a risk by entering this twelfth-century Norse construction, built when Kirkwall was still a village under Viking rule. I stopped trying to learn about British history once I got up to about AD 900, so it was a learning curve for me to realize that Viking influence remained very strong in the north centuries later.

After all this culture, we lacked the stamina to actually go inside the beautiful Italian Chapel, but it looked a bit like a white dolls' house from the outside as we chose to sit on the coach and munch some grub. Our fellow coach-trippers returned full of enthusiasm, but we were done for the day. Sadly, after looking it up recently, I finally realize what a stunning place I missed out on! It turns out that about five hundred Italian prisoners of war were brought from North Africa to Orkney in the 1940s to work as labourers on the Churchill barriers. These were being set up to stop ships trying to approach Scapa Flow from the east, and the workers needed a chapel for worship. According to the bus-driver, the weather was the best he had seen all year. Maybe I should not have been surprised, since I had actually begun the day by asking God to get rid of the clouds!

Would anyone like to know three useless facts about Orkney? Well, here they are anyway. Surprisingly, fifty-nine out of the seventy islands are uninhabited, and the overall population is only about twenty thousand. I noticed a reluctance on the part of the population about being referred to as Scots; they preferred to call themselves "the people of Orkney". It felt very relaxing, and we both really enjoyed the day.

Dad left, and I continued on to Wick. John O'Groats now lay just a day's walk away, and a sense of eager expectation consumed me. On finally reaching this north-eastern corner of mainland Britain, I was initially overcome with a sense of personal satisfaction. The welcome thought struck me that for the first time I could now walk west instead of exclusively north, which had felt so much like going away from home for the last three months. To describe it as a milestone would be to understate what was going on inside of me. Despite knowing that I still had two-thirds of the journey ahead, it really felt that I had somehow made it. Even if I had to turn back now, through some unforeseeable disaster, I had still achieved something unlikely to be repeated by any of my friends or family. I could still hear one or two voices from the recent past telling me that I would never make it beyond John O'Groats. But phase one was well and truly over, and in fact there was no desire to turn back.

It was a pity that John O'Groats wasn't much more to look at than a grotty old signpost showing distances to various other places. You could pay a fortune to have your photo taken beside the signpost displaying the distance to your home town, but I declined, and focused on striding out towards Dunnet Head – the "really" most northerly part of mainland Britain.

Thurso, Melvich, Bettyhill, Tongue, Eriboll = 77 miles

Thurso Church happened to be one of my favourite churches on the entire walk. I'm not usually very partial to super-long services. We kicked off at around 6.30 p.m. and continued until past nine, but no-one batted an eyelid. The worship itself went on for about an hour and a half. Virtually everyone seemed to be entering in to it. There were a number crying and down on their knees, as God's Spirit moved across the meeting. We sang one of my favourite songs again and again for about fifteen minutes. What a beauty!

> "Here is love, vast as the ocean; loving-kindness as the flood.
> When the Prince of life, our ransom, shed for us His
>   precious blood.
> Who His love will not remember?
> Who can cease to sing His praise?
> He can never be forgotten throughout heaven's eternal days."

The following morning, I left for Melvich on quite a high. My host John, along with Ruby from a different church, joined me as we prayed around a run-down housing estate. We decided to pop in on a dear old lady who at that exact moment had been wondering how we were getting on. We prayed with her, and moved on through the vicious clegs (Scottish horse-flies) who had turned out in force to welcome Scotland's hottest day of the year thus far. Man alive, their silent ambushes annoy and hurt!

As John and Ruby said goodbye, another new friend turned up and continued the journey. Mark was to join me for walking and praying more than once during the week, and stayed in frequent contact for about a month thereafter. When Eriboll neared, two guys introduced themselves to me. They saw my back pack, I saw theirs, and our paths were immediately drawn together. Both looked war-torn and battered. They'd been walking from Land's End to John O'Groats, and had almost completed their journey. One of them couldn't get over how well I looked after having travelled so far. You couldn't help but notice the look on their faces as they realized that their journey was but a small slice of what mine would become! Bless them, they were in awe of an ordinary guy who had been given an extraordinary mission. I told them that my strength came from God, and sensed that they believed me.

Durness, Scourie, Lochinver, Altandhu = 88 miles

You don't really get to see much sign of life on the north coast of Scotland even in July. I'm speaking of human life by the way, because God's creation is quite stunning up this way. The scenery itself seems to be able to communicate with the spirit. Don't worry, I haven't been talking to trees yet, but I have come close! The scattered population is found mostly in small villages, where the simple crofter's lifestyle continues as it has done for centuries, still bubbling with life!

I could go for days without seeing a soul, so it came as a pleasant surprise when Johnny and Joyce pulled up alongside and gestured me inside their nearby home. Initially this was for a cup of tea but it soon turned into sandwiches and tasty homemade shortbread biscuits. A glance at the bookshelf confirmed my hunch that they had to be Christians. At the same time I had the feeling that Johnny was figuring me out. It didn't take long for us to be more than comfortable in one another's company. Minutes later, we were praying for revival in our nation, and I ended up staying for a couple of hours. This was fine, because that day's walk was shortish anyway, and it rained the whole time I was in the house!

Not long after I got out of their door, I ended up at the youth hostel and shared my testimony with a Buddhist. It was at this time that I met some of the most fantastic people so far

– fellow travellers, shall we say? Not Christians to my knowledge, but really nice friends. Most without homes, they just permanently travelled, and had some amazing values about human life and its preciousness! We started a little chess tournament – Kent won two of the three matches. Thanks for coming!

Huh, midges! I'd heard about them, and now I was beginning to feel them, the rascals! Talk about hunting in packs! Man, do those things follow you everywhere you go! I found out one challenging way of keeping them away! Ready for it! *Avon Skin So Soft*. You end up smelling like a girl, and getting some funny looks in the pubs, but it works pretty well.

> "The completion of Gary's walk is a wonderful achievement, particularly on his part, but also his whole back-up team. It was good to meet Gary in Lochinver and to hear some of his experiences. We look forward to reading more in the book. What particularly impressed us about Gary was his willingness to spend some time kicking a ball about with some of our young people in the Leisure Centre, after a long day walking. He was a great example to them of a love of life, and a wholesome enthusiasm."
>
> ***Rosemary***

Ullapool, Braemore, Ardessie, Aultbea = 69 miles

The day before I reached Ullapool, I had a shocker. It was wet, the hills were steep and I had eighteen miles to cover. So, it was more than a blessing when my host drove alongside and relieved me of my rucksack with a few light miles remaining. Organized people would have made sure to get their GPS out before handing the rucksack over. But as I didn't, my walk became a marathon in the heavy rain, and my guessing skills let me down whenever I found a signpost. I met only two people, both of whom were thankfully able to give me directions.

So it was no surprise that, as I woke next morning to the sound of more heavy rain, there were aches in every part of my body. The previous day's torrents had completely penetrated my waterproof rucksack, spare clothes and all, despite my highly original extra precautions with black sacks. My hosts' best drying attempts over-night having proved ineffectual, I faced a fifteen-miler in clothes that were already wet! Good Christians would have taken it all in their stride, but I'm not wired that way. I couldn't help feeling hard done by. Didn't God know that I needed a hot windy day? I unleashed a hurl of unsavoury abuse His way, ridden with guilt as I did so, and ending up feeling ten times worse. It had completely slipped my mind that just a day earlier I had been praying for patience!

On the way to Aultbea, I encountered more than one herd of wild goats, plus many a wandering sheep, which made me feel sorry for motorists having to dodge these sporadic hazards. I've become quite a fan of watching birds, especially raptors, and there were plenty of buzzards and sea eagles about. Walking along the road to the harbour, you can also see man's work – moorings for large vessels, facilitating Aultbea's role as a NATO refuelling location. My preference would have been to hunt out the hairy armpit tree in nearby Bamboo Salem, but time ran out on me yet again.

Gairloch, Kinlochewe, Sheildag, Lochcarron = 64 miles

During my visit to Gairloch, I was unaware that it would become the central location for the 2007 BBC One match-making series When Love Comes to Town. Guess my timing was eighteen months out. The local tourist office boast is: "If you've seen Gairloch, you've seen the Highlands." This claim is less wild than it seems, since the area possibly does have a bit of most things that attract visitors to the Highlands. The coastline is alternately rocky and sandy, and includes islands, a lighthouse and fishing boats, plus incredible views of nearby mountains. The village itself is strung out, and closely connected with the sea, whilst the Flowerdale Burn hosts yet another extremely impressive Scottish waterfall. Can you believe that out of a population of five hundred, over one hundred and fifty attended the church I was with that Sunday? It would be interesting to know the overall national percentage of churchgoers! Can anywhere beat Gairloch? It was the type of village where everyone knew each other. You got the feeling that the door was always open for a cuppa. The atmosphere was one of peace, and you could feel God's close presence.

The next morning as I was listening to my MP3 player on the way to Kinlochewe a camper van pulled over, and it was packed full. They were having a wager as to what kind of music I was clearly enjoying. Rock? Indie? Punk? Jazz? Pop? A big smile broke out on the face of the twelve-year-old boy who had guessed rock, when I said that it was Christian rock music. I ended up having quite a good conversation with those travellers.

It was at Lochcarron that I saw my first eagle since setting off; it was massive! I wouldn't exactly call myself a bird watcher, but its wing span was unbelievable. By way of a rare treat, I had learned that it was raining in Kent, and sunny here, and I was sinfully glad to hear it!

Kyle of Lochalsh, Armadale, Mallaig, Fort William = 50 miles

Kyle of Lochalsh itself didn't impress me all that greatly. It wasn't until I caught my first glimpse of the Isle of Skye that I realized that I was about to see some of the best scenery in Britain.

I have heard that the Gaelic language has been undergoing a recent revival in some parts, which had obviously reached Skye quite a long time back. Vincent and Michael had a long, traffic-jammed drive before they squeezed onto the last ferry from Mallaig. Unfortunately for them they didn't get to see Skye in all its glory, as it rained for the next two days. I was gutted for them. There was nowhere dry to talk, so Vincent and I stopped off at a café, where we made our one cup of tea last for as long as we could, but ended up outstaying our welcome and were politely invited to move on from the busy overflowing café!

It was so beautiful on Skye, and people were so relaxed about security, that it was quite a shock to discover that crime existed here like everywhere else. I heard direct from relatives of a poor guy who had been brutally savaged by a drunken nut-case. He ended up with every bone in his face broken. With our knees knocking, we prayed hastily around the area and got out quickly. We were to hear later from Mary that our feeble prayers had been answered.

Seal Island was dotted with enormous brown sluggish animals, including a large number of pups, though to me they simply looked like grey blobs. The island resembled a giant cow pat, a pretty barren hideout for seals, and perhaps a bit of a disappointment after what we had seen in the publicity. The boat bobbed up and down so fast, it was hard to keep the camera still. Most of the seals were white with black blotches. It is a good job that their coats are waterproof, and a pity that the video camera didn't have similar protection, as the rain was coming down in sheets.

Chris was so fascinated by train 62005, as it belched disgusting pollution into the pure air on its way to Mallaig, that he almost got run over by a car as he stood drooling. Behind him Ben Nevis looked on, and chuckled soundlessly. Our walk consisted of climbing countless Monroes, with endless spurts of water continually flowing downwards.

Whenever we stopped for a nibble we were set on by midges, even hungrier than ourselves, and passionate about the English flesh. It didn't stop us having a great time of prayer and worship though.

Glencoe, Bridge of Orchy, Dalmally, Inveraray = 74 miles

Climbing towards Bridge of Orchy, I met two Aussies. One of these ladies was training for the ministry, so I told them about the walk, and its purpose. They were both highly impressed, but I can't recall the Aussie equivalent words which they used. Unwittingly flattering my good looks, they both insisted on numerous photos to take home and show their mates. Their enthusiasm for male Poms in general may have been dampened if they had been able to foresee the butt-whipping which awaited their beloved Ponting and his over-rated first eleven the very next day! Personally I relished every moment, and thought about the stick those ministers would get from the English contingent staying at their hotel. Let's just pass over the 2006/7 Ashes series, otherwise known as Ponting's Revenge!

You would be surprised if you knew how I kept up-to-date with the fall of wickets. I had no idea that the Scots were so keen on watching English test cricket. It was easy to keep peeping through windows as I devotedly prayer-walked, hmmm! I felt the joy of the Lord as England knocked off the runs. I went from viewing cricket through windows to sitting down that evening bawling my eyes out whilst watching *Philadelphia*.

More than once I unintentionally flirted with Tarbet's hidden mysteries, as I felt the soggy embrace of its mud flats, whose stickily irresistible kisses temporarily sucked the boots from my unwilling feet. By the time I could regain them, those clogs were soaked, smelly, coal black and unwearable. The most disgusting thing of all was putting them back on, and continuing the journey knowing that the mud flats had left such marks of affection with me! Every step I took for the next ten miles would include another slobbery kiss for my poor feet!

Rowandennan, Auchdennan, Dumbarton, Glasgow = 67 miles

I had the MP3 on all day as I listened to worship, trekking over the Monroes, and through woods towards Rowandennan. It got a bit marshy in places, and I thought that I was going to sink in mud more than once, but somehow the boots survived this time, despite attempting to yank themselves from my feet yet again.

There wasn't a soul in sight all day – no surprise there, then! I stopped off at the pub for dinner, and met Colin and Jan from Charlton. What a lovely couple! We sat there and put the world to rights for a while, talking especially about immigrants, and how they were not so keen on them. When I shared about the idea of the walk, they asked if I'd always been a Christian, so I shared my story of coming to know God. Neither of them had a Christian faith, but both were interested in spiritual things. Jan had been to a spiritualist meeting, and was impacted by it. It was a great time, and they kindly bought me a beer as they left.

The fantastically beautiful walk down the side of Loch Lomond was followed by a first-class ferry ride across breath-takingly still waters. When God looks first at such wonders of His handiwork, and then at us, do the former really pale into insignificance because He places more value on us as the masterpiece of creation? Yes sirree!

Psalm 8 asks,

> "What is man, that you are mindful of him? . . .
> You made him ruler over the works of your hands."

(vv. 4, 6)

I wonder whether betting shops are the works of His hands. From my experience from around Glasgow – no! I felt God draw me inside more than one solely to pray, and every one of them was heaving, and full of the sad faces of men and women gripped by an uncontrollable lust for money. It became so clear to me that we are at our best when we worship God, rather than wealth. Love of money has resulted in so many suicides, broken marriages, wrecked lives, and – at the very least – a purposeless existence. Money disappoints, God fulfills!

It was an easy flight from Prestwick to Gatwick, and then just an hour's drive to Ashburnham where I spent a great week off with the youth and other friends from my home church.

Largs, Kilmarnock, Prestwick, Maybole = 82 miles

After that quality sunny week off, the first day back on the road saw the most rain I had yet experienced in a single twenty-four hour period. Thank you, Murphy and your sodden law! The physical side of walking was really hard – although the break had been relatively short – because my fitness level had dropped. But I was on a spiritual high, and at least it was easy to pray. The back-up team had arranged a B & B for me in Kilmarnock, but I had arrived too early, and the house was empty. As I hesitated on the doorstep the lady from next door (or was she an angel?) called me in for a bowl of delicious soup, coffee and biscuits!

I let myself down earlier by not offering to pray for a guy on crutches, but I was encouraged to hear from Luke that my walk website was receiving at least 5,500 hits a month. I found myself on some sort of dog walkers' circuit as I trekked towards Maybole, dodging their occasional misdemeanour whilst having good conversations with their owners. If you ever want to build friendships from scratch, maybe you should try getting yourself a dog.

Dreams are very rare for me, unless I have consumed considerable amounts of cheese, and I mean bucket-loads of the stuff. So it came as a big surprise to be sleeping, and thinking about eagles. I dreamt of a bright blue eagle soaring in the sky, huge and beautiful, out of reach, but still very visible. It swooped down and caught another bird of prey unawares having come from such a height, and at lightning speed. It devoured its victim, and left ready for the next catch. For the next few days I kept thinking about that dream. I had no idea what it meant, and still don't, but I kept seeing eagles. They were everywhere – on mantlepieces, in the sky, in the distance. At Prestwick Airport I even saw a statue of a human with eagles' wings.

> "Gary's visit was a wonderful opportunity to gather neighbours together, and tell them about our faith. People resistant to the Bible will not visit a church, but they will come to an event in the home, to hear about a walk around our country. Gary's talk reinforced our witness with stories of people he met. Some asked for prayer, which was an encouragement to us. It is many months now since he came, but people still ask 'How is Gary getting on?' So his visit clearly had impact."
>
> *John and Mary*

Girvan, Ballantrae, Glenluce = 48 miles

As was the case most Sundays, I was let loose to share about the walk – this time from the front of the busy Scottish Presbyterian Church at Girvan. Pastor Doug decided to interview me, so as to stop me rambling on. It went so well that the congregation wanted to meet me again that evening, when amazingly they survived until gone eleven. My friends tell me it's obvious that my listeners were bored so rigid they were unable to leave, but at least I enjoyed myself.

How would you feel if you were walking all by yourself and you were accosted by a tank of an Irish trucker? As I was stopping for lunch en route to Ballantrae, a great big juggernaut stopped alongside me, and its big brute of a driver invited me to hop up alongside him. He was extravagantly tattooed, double my Mr Incredible build, every other word was unprintable, his voice was deep and husky, and the Irish brogue was so strong that I struggled to understand two words together. After listening to his story, although I was brickin' 'em inside, I somehow found myself saying I was a Christian. Looking back, I can't believe how brave I was that day.

Instead of being angered by my mention of Jesus, this guy seemed to completely soften. It turned out that his ex-druggie brother had been completely transformed as a result of becoming a Christian. My new friend opened right up, and shared about some stuff which he now regrets doing. He has been to court fourteen times so far, in a desperate effort to be allowed to see his kids. Humanly speaking, it is a brick wall. So I took his case to the divine court in prayer and hopped out, no further on in the journey, and hardly able to believe what had just happened.

Newton Stewart, Gatehouse of Fleet, Kirkcudbright, Castle Douglas = 53 miles

Gatehouse of Fleet became a town about three hundred years ago, and before long cotton mills sprang up everywhere. My walk being people-centred, there was no time to visit Cardoness Castle, which swaggers over the town to the west on the original coastline. Six storeys tall, it was originally built by the McCulloch clan, whose family history seems particularly violent even for those times. They originally got the estate when a McCulloch married the youngest daughter of the previous landowner. Apparently she had eight elder sisters, so when a baby boy was eventually born there was a big party, but her excited father took the other eight girls and the baby out on a frozen lake to celebrate. Unfortunately, everyone suddenly disappeared forever through the ice.

Another McCulloch was imprisoned for stealing from his widowed mother, and for generations the family was notorious for violent assaults on neighbours. Gambling debts led to the eventual sale of the castle, but family members still thought it was theirs. As a result, the new owner's widow was thrown onto a dung heap by a deranged McCulloch in 1668, and a generation later her son was murdered by Sir Godfrey McCulloch. Makes the present age seem fairly peaceful, doesn't it?

I'm embarrassed to confess that my encyclopedia of personal knowledge previously excluded the fact that clockwork mechanisms were invented in the 1770s by Robert Williamson. It was an additional surprise to learn that he set up a workshop in this relatively isolated town. Not that this story ends too happily either, since the workshop burned to the ground with him inside it before the end of the decade!

It seems that most towns have a reason behind their names, and this one was no exception. At nearby Fleet Bay, the river known as "Water of Fleet" flows out into the sea. The town itself sort of guards a vital point on the eighteenth-century stagecoach route from Dumfries to Stranraer. Nowadays this road is the fairly safe A75, but back then it was a hazardous journey, and travellers preferred an overnight stay at the "Gait" to risking a night-time encounter with highwaymen or local bandits.

It's a pity, too, not to have known that I was just a mile from Aworth, where Samuel Rutherford, the well-known Puritan preacher, was based from 1627 to 1636. A visit could have been really uplifting, which was food for thought along the road to Castle Douglas, known as Carlingwark until 1792, when Sir William Douglas designed a new, very orderly village plan to replace the old. At first the new town was able to produce handspun cotton profitably, before water-powered mills became the rage. However, the number of hotels built at the time shows that the town was popular as a safe highway stopover, and in 1900 Castle Douglas was the largest market town around. If only you could retain this kind of information just by soaking in the atmosphere of the place. As it is, within a couple of years I'll have to read my own book in order to find all this out again!

Much more Indiana Jones territory lay ahead, and yet more mud stuck to those boots. One thing is for sure – I have more samples of British cow pat on my boots than pigs manage to roll around in a lifetime. Back home, Peter and Lesley had faithfully kept their long-standing promise to arrange for me to spend a weekend with their friends in Castle Douglas, where I had a great time.

Brian and Reena really helped me to feel relaxed in their home. I interviewed Brian on the video camera which was interesting since we come from opposite ends of the belief spectrum. Destiny vs chance, creation vs evolution, instinct vs emotions, life after death vs extinction, God vs no God. In the middle of our debate I felt as if I was getting nowhere. God dropped into my mind the need to be personal, so I started asking Brian why he loves, where hate comes from, etc.? Brian then asked me to be "not so personal", so I knew that God had found a way of communicating with him. We then went inside, turned on the TV, and the first words we heard were "And the Lord said let there be light and there was light!" Cool!

"Good luck with the book, although I don't think you need luck. Take care of yourself and if you are this way again call and see us."

Rena and Brian

Dumfries, Annan, Carlisle, Cockermouth = 77 miles

Listening to God can be quite a difficult conundrum. Half the time you think you are making it up. You start telling yourself the right things to do, and then say that it was God suggesting it. Or else, the thoughts are so random it couldn't possibly be God, though God did tell people in the Bible to do some strange stuff. Would you wipe mud in someone's eyes, or hit a stone with a stick to get water? So when I thought I heard this inner voice saying that God was currently running a tape measure around Dumfries, because what He was going to do was great, and would cover all of it, I didn't immediately write it off. Then came one of those moments of confirmation that you treasure; as I turned the corner of the road, some way off I could see two men measuring a big distance. Coincidence? Yes, but one that God had arranged so as to communicate with me.

> "Gary is a fine young man who went down a treat in the Annan manse, where my two daughters thought he was cool, handsome, etc., and definitely not weird like so many of Dad's Christian friends! Gary also watched the England Northern Ireland football match, along with my three teenage children. Naturally, since they belonged to the old enemy, we were all cheering for Northern Ireland, the eventual winners. Gary took it with the grace and charm of a true gent."
>
> *Yours aye, Hugh*

Talking of distances, my host John was the only person I met who could outdo me in terms of miles walked in prayer. He has clocked up over 6,000 miles so far, wheeling a big cross which God has used many times to draw people to Himself. John tells stories of people running out of pubs falling on their knees and crying at the foot of the cross, while others pinned their prayer requests to it. For John it was a burden, but one that was worth carrying.

Thank you, Scotland. Of the three British countries included in my walk, I completed your spectacular coastline first! I stood at the signpost in Gretna for a while trying to take it all in, remembering a whole host of special people, amazing views, lots of rain, huge hills, miracles, pubs, friends, trials, temptations, God's provision, strength, empowering care, and the list goes on.

On the way to Cockermouth, I had to trim a few miles off a thirty mile walk, so I let the train take the strain for a bit. As I was getting off, God gave me a word for a guy who looked quite trapped and alone. I knew from what he was wearing that he was a Muslim, and I also knew that God's message for him was simple – "Jesus wants you in His family!" His face lit up, and as I walked along the platform I saw him reading the gospel tract I left with him.

I met Phil and Maggie in Cockermouth. Phil was a keen prayer-walker who also carried a cross whilst walking – that was two in three days. I left him John's details, along with the book he gave me.

> "It was great to have Gary staying here in Cockermouth. He was a great inspiration to us."
>
> *Phil and Maggie*

Maryport, Whitehaven, Beckermet, Bootle = 46 miles

Whilst walking towards not-so-nice Maryport (sorry!) I bumped into a guy called Ayrton, who was to join me for the rest of the day's stroll. Ayrton was a keen rambler, and he was chatting about all the weird and wonderful places he had visited. It came to me to ask him whether he had ever thought about praying whilst walking. That was a notion that he could not quite cotton on to, his idea being that God simply made the world and left us to get on with it. So he was intrigued as I shared very directly about being able to have a down-to-earth relationship with God. He was really interested, happily took the tract I offered him, and asked me to stay in contact. Whoops, sorry! If you are reading this and want to regain touch, details are in this book.

On the way to Whitehaven, the south-westerly gales left my hair in spiky knots as they whistled towards the Scottish border which I had left behind five days before. By this time my hair had reached "Cousin It" proportions – and that was just on my chin! Near St Bees, I found myself surrounded by talkative members of the Keswick Rambling Club. Their enthusiasm was overwhelming, as they took innumerable photos, and insisted on adding me to their website.

The original plan for me to stay in a youth hostel, inland and off-route, got to be changed. Special thanks to Peter and Joelle in Beckermet, friends of Peter and Maggie, for putting up a complete stranger right at the last minute. To think that they had just a few days to prepare for my arrival is mind-boggling!

Coniston, Windermere, Kendal, Kirkby Lonsdale = 55 miles

Coniston existed as just another village community set in the amazing scenery of Lakeland, until a hundred and fifty years ago, when its existing copper mines were completely regenerated. Many tourists reckon that its best feature is the huge hill known as "The Old Man of Coniston" which suddenly appears from behind the houses as you pass through the centre of the village.

It was on Coniston Water that Donald Campbell gained the world water-speed record in the 1920s. Sadly, it was in the same place that, trying to get the record back, he met his

death in 1967. His memorial on the village green continues
to attract visitors. Not until 8th March 2001 was his boat,
Bluebird, raised from the lake bed, and a couple more months
passed before his actual remains were brought up for burial in
the local graveyard. Strange to think that so many people I
know remember this incident like yesterday. For me it is like a
bit of history, having been born more than a decade after
Campbell met his untimely end.

John Fudge, a good mate from back home, joined me for a
day to climb some of the steepest Cumbrian hills. He is a big
noise in Crusaders nationally, and part of my home church.
We talked about vision, and what we wanted God to do in
our day. Our heart-cry is to see breakthrough in this entire
generation. There are plenty of mice out to play, but we want
to hear the lion roar.

Next day, Alan took me on an unexpected trip to a local
hiking shop. I'd had another of my Indiana Jones adventures,
finding my way rudely barred by an enormous spiky peri-
meter fence. It was too high for me to launch my rucksack
over in advance, so with that crushing load on my back I
somehow scaled the nearest tree to spy out the land. Once
I had reached the heavens, my all-seeing eye perceived a
branch hanging over the top of the fence. Tarzan-like, I
grabbed it and swung myself into the unknown! I came down
to earth quite literally with a thud. Cor, that was a ground-
breaking experience. As I reviewed what had happened in the
previous twenty minutes, it became clear to me that the many
obstacles around meant I had been somehow out of bounds,
and I breathed a sigh of relief that it was all over. Having
escaped Alcatraz, one single, insignificant barrier stood
between myself and total freedom. Scaling a puny, semi-
derelict metal fence seemed like nothing compared with my
recent exploits, even if it was topped by a trail of rusting
barbed wire – no problems! I had hopped over plenty worse
than that in the course of the last five months. All I had to do

was repeat the same approach – put one leg part way up, use it as a foundation to climb another rung, and safely over and away. Not this time though, hence Alan and the hiking shop. New gear needed!

Morecambe, Blackpool, Preston, Southport = 74 miles

You don't often catch me up bright and early, but being on Jim and Catherine's farm meant that I had a chance to see cows being milked by getting myself into their cow shed by 6.30 in the morning. Not that I was born in the Stone Age, but I had this hazy childhood idea that Jim would be perched on a stool over a bucket, squeezing in all the right places. So it came as a massive culture shock to find myself encircled by computerized precision machinery, all perfectly managed by Jim. In the time I would have thought it would have needed to milk one cow manually, he had handled at least ten. Another learning curve for the Lamb!

It was absolutely great to pray at night from the top of Blackpool Tower, along with a group of new friends. We kept going, whether we were alone or not! Unfortunately my delight was beginning to be overshadowed by some persistent back pain, which I realized was not going to simply disappear. My day had already included a fifteen-mile drudge carrying a heavy rucksack on a hurting back. No sensible person would have finished it by climbing that cruel stairway, but then – as most of you know – I'm stark raving bonkers! I ended up having my rucksack transported from host to host for the next couple of days, courtesy of Graham Burke, whose family hosted me magnificently. Church on the Sunday was spontaneously led as the pastor called for any person needing to be baptized. A girl responded, and to my pleased astonishment it was done there and then.

God really is moving, but it seems to be in pockets, here and there. Of course we want the massive stuff. But take Ian and Nadia who are part of a church plant in Preston that started from scratch two years ago. They now have eighty-five on a Sunday morning. Brand new Christians as well, straight from the streets, with no spiritual background! They are in fact so new that they are refreshing. They shared about one girl who asked to be on the welcoming team, because she had a heart to make people feel at home. She arrived for her welcoming duties in a low-cut top, mini skirt, ciggy in one hand, and mobile in the other! Now, the leaders bring a bucket of sand each week for the cigarette butts, so they don't litter the streets. People from all walks of life come in, and get saved. The church loves the person first, then behaviour change soon follows. If it doesn't, it doesn't – so what?

Liverpool, Runcorn, Eastham = 54 miles

As a keen supporter of the Reds, you might think I would have been really well up on Liverpool's local history, but I have to admit it came as a surprise to find the city sprawled across a ridge of hills. It was also news to me that 2002 government records showed it to be England's fifth most populated city, and of course I had never heard before that the nickname "scousers" comes from a popular local stew.

How many of my readers know that not much more than a century ago Liverpool was known as "the second port of the British Empire", controlling nearly 15% of the world's shipping? As I write, the city is about to celebrate its 800th anniversary, and is soon to be the proud bearer of the title "European Capital of Culture" for a year. It was exciting to find that the new pier terminal will allow a ship as large as the QE2 to dock there. Some of my mates are maybe stuck with a completely wrong image of Liverpool, which from what I could see is now a city of amazing views and excellent modern developments.

However, you could barely move in Wavertree without wondering how it must feel to be imprisoned for a crime when you believe yourself to be not guilty. Every pub window in sight carried a Michael Shields poster declaring his innocence, and calling for his release. I saw quite a few smashed up windows and broken down houses, and it was a relief to reach my hosts unscathed. My hosts in Liverpool told me about some miracles they had seen recently, including the healing of a deaf man, and that now they had been saving up some mustard seeds and putting them in bottles to give to people, in connection with Jesus' words telling us that he who has faith as small as a mustard seed can move mountains. I was given a few to share out on my journey.

After a day hosted by Liverpool Frontline Church, which has a kids' club of over four hundred, it really was a case of from large to little, as I found myself in Runcorn with a Baptist Church no bigger than the Walton household. But they both felt like family.

"It was a joy to have Gary with us in Runcorn for the night, and to hear him talk with David about football! We are glad that he has had some company along what could have been a very lonely way. Please give our love to Gary's family, and tell them that we really enjoyed his short stay, and giving him his favourite breakfast. Bacon butties!"

Margaret, Eddy and David

The first time I saw Don and Paul they were toiling uphill with their bikes, trailing in the wake of my giant "go go Gadget" strides. Moments later, as the terrain changed in their favour, I became aware of their breath on my shoulder as they drew level. We ended up somehow chatting about Fred, a seriously ill friend of theirs. In my pocket was my bottle of mustard seeds, which God had told me to use as a faith challenge. I handed them three, encouraging them to pass one on to their cancer-stricken buddy. I knew God was there because they seemed to treasure what I had given them, first clutching the seeds, and then carefully storing them away. They then breezed effortlessly into the lead, and the last I saw of them was their backs, as they headed towards the imaginary finishing line somewhere just down the road.

Hoylake, Queensferry, Flint = 50 miles

Hoylake was the scene of my encounters with blind people which you can read about in chapter 6. Happily, although I was a bit weak regarding other people's eyes, at least my own spiritual ears had been working. God had spoken to me about the effect of the mustard seeds I had been given, and I knew that He wanted me to use some prophetically on my forth-coming home visit.

The problem was I had completely run out. So I abandoned my GPS and threw myself on God's direction. I felt drawn to go down a random road entirely unconnected to the straight-forward route. Within fifteen minutes I was inside a garden centre.

It was good to learn for the first time (!) of the existence of William Gladstone. Apparently he was prime minister four times in the late nineteenth century, and also had a vision for bringing together scholars who would search for Christian truth, a process he described as divine learning. Towards this, he founded St Deiniol's, the only residential library in the UK. I am told that he was a voracious reader who devoured about twenty thousand books in his lifetime, but I was grateful to make use of his library for its other main purpose – simply somewhere inexpensive to rest my weary limbs. It actually turned out to be extremely comfortable. Nat was there with me for a night, and we both felt that St Deiniol's luxuries were only matched by the excellence of the meal we enjoyed just round the corner at The Fox and Grapes. Suitably refreshed, Nat and I set off next day towards Flint, the last port of call before my fourth home break. Nat's mum, Eileen, kindly saved me from a tricky train journey by giving us both a lift back to Kent.

Prestatyn, Llandudno, Bangor = 56 miles

Being separated again from friends and family, and returning to solitude, was a hard pill to swallow. The routine of daily distance walking would need to be re-built. My break had lasted a mere four days, but my limbs were feeling it, as I trundled into action. I was a bag of unwilling bones creaking towards Prestatyn. One thing was for sure, it was good to get off the greasy take-aways, and back on to quality banquets, exchanging my own unwashed crusty sheets at home for freshly made double beds.

Who says that human kindness doesn't exist these days? Les is involved in an initiative which has a simple aim. With God's help, they fix families. The project is like a little housing estate for broken lives, and has room for up to thirty-five parents and their kids. It made me think – why hasn't every area got one? There is such a demand for this kind of care in every community. All the basic needs were met for what the world would call "no-hopers". If anyone out there has some money, what about that for an idea?

In general, my health remained remarkably good for the whole ten months of the walk. Through baking sun, freezing conditions, drenching rain, miserable fog, and howling gales my body stayed obstinately robust. But Wales came closest to defeating me! It all started in Bangor, with the onset of a cold that I thought would be easy to shake off. But it was to be twenty-five days before I could finally record my recovery in blog, and for quite a lot of that time I had to keep going against stomach cramps, vomiting, aching bones, heavy sniffles, tight chest, and the list goes on! And so to Anglesey.

Benllech, Cemaes, Holyhead, Holy Island, Newborough = 62 miles

Everyone says that the view from the Menai Bridge going over into Anglesey is unforgettably magnificent. How sad is it that I can't remember a thing about it! Benllech saw me sleep actually in St Andrews Church, in a camp bed on the church floor. It had a calming presence, and amazingly I slept as well there as I did in many a more comfy double bed elsewhere. The church had arranged free food for me at the local café, where I had an unusual opportunity to show the love of God in a practical way. A young lady with a small child had forgotten her purse, and was negotiating how to pay the next day. Over-hearing this, I felt moved to pay the bill for her. She was highly embarrassed but also deeply touched by my act of kindness, which I think she will not forget. It was a great chance to talk about the walk. The rain was slogging down as Andy Hughes (Wales Crusaders big wig) and I squelched our way to Cemaes. Andy kept praying away despite the torrential downpours. We got completely lost as we clambered despairingly over broken stiles and fences, avoiding cows as we tried to follow a footpath that was clearly marked on the GPS, although apparently no-one had remembered to tell the farmer about maintaining it. To crown it all, having finally located the anticipated warm, luxurious, welcoming pub which we had earmarked for lunch, we found ourselves confronted by an old, semi boarded up, ill-kept building. With little hope, we attempted to enter but every door was locked. By now you know that my courage can be increased in proportion to the volume of my hunger pangs. So you will not be surprised to learn two minutes later we were disturbing the peace of the nearest house. Get in there! Sam came up trumps with some tasty sandwiches, which I ate with some difficulty as my hands were literally shaking with cold.

It was really great walking round Holy Island, or Ynys Cybi as the Welsh call it. Given a bit more time, one could have checked out this saint Cybi, who apparently actually gave up inheriting the kingdom of Cornwall in order to tell people in Wales about Jesus. It's also said that he acquired a real face colouring because – on his frequent visits to his friend saint Seinon – he always liked to walk facing the sun, and became known as St Cybi the tanned one.

Presumably the climate in North Wales at that time was different from my own rain-soaked experiences in autumn 2005, apart from this one-off day!

With a total population of under 14,000, the island has a sense of spaciousness and rest. Perhaps it is this sense of peacefulness which encouraged the inhabitants of North Wales, centuries back, to construct the large number of standing stones, religious sites and burial chambers dotted all over the area. One of my favourite photos from the walk is of the South Stack lighthouse. There are so many tiny islands and stacks around Holy Island, plus dangerous cliffs and jagged shoreline rocks. It's hard to imagine how local ships could have sailed safely at all before the lighthouse was built.

Caernarfon, Trefor, Tudweiliog = 87 miles

Having just left Llanfairpwllgwyngyllgogerychwyrndrobwll-llantysiliogogogoch behind on Anglesey, it was quite a relief to come to somewhere whose name I could at least have a go at pronouncing.

No matter how hard I tried zooming out, I could not get the whole name to fit on my camera screen.

A great shock came my way when mum emailed my phone to say that my nan was receiving treatment following a heart attack. I felt so helpless – I wanted so much to get to see her, but if I was to walk direct by motorway at my average daily speed it would be three weeks later before I made it, though of course I knew someone would come and get me if necessary. It came as a comfort to find out that she was being treated by a mate of mine, who was a Christian.

The local *Chronicle* did a really good write up on my walk, although I found it rather strange to feature on page three. I did wonder if they thought I was the naked rambler in disguise. Walking towards Tudwelly-dog a stray canine friend latched itself onto me like the remains of scrambled egg on an unwashed plate. It's a bit sad, but I really enjoyed our brief time together. The nervous tension induced by watching him flirt with death under the wheels of oncoming traffic left me both exhilarated and exhausted. The severing of our relationship came, as so often happens, with the intrusion of a third party. This took the form of a dashing mongrel, who immediately attempted a close clinch with my companion. Sadly, the latter instantly deserted me for the better model, and I continued on life's journey, temporarily desolate and bereaved.

Abersoch, Criccieth, Llanbedr = 44 miles

It was in Abersoch that I stayed with my first South African couple. Jack and Carlien succeeded in whetting my appetite by setting before me a South African delicacy which tasted like sweet dumplings. I could have quite easily polished off their plates as well as mine. Very tasty!

It was great to have the opportunity to repay Luke in a small way. Every day he managed my website, and now he was asking me to pray for his sick daughter. Luke was over the moon about God's quick answer to my prayer, and the very next night the whole family slept well.

I was halfway between Criccieth and Llanbedr and about ready to replenish the Lamb gut with a bit of lunch, when I felt that I should carry on for a bit. The reason for this became clear when after about another mile or so I met Gail. As was so often the case in Wales it was tipping it down with rain, but all we did was to stand still and get soaked to the skin while we chatted for a good ten minutes. It was so rewarding later that night to receive confirmation by email that it had all been worthwhile and God had been at work in Gail's heart. Her message started with these words:

> "Thank you for brightening my day with your friendly face, your pure vitality, your marvellous radiance, and talk of your walk."

Things hadn't been going well for Gail recently, but through our conversation God had helped her gain clarity in her life.

Over a long weekend, my host Dave – an excellent photographer – gave me a pictorial preview of stunning locations I would be visiting shortly.

Dolgellau, Fairbourne, Aberdyfi, Machynlleth = 53 miles

Tom and Nick, a couple of lads from the church youth club, joined me as we got to taste the horizontal Welsh rain. We kept getting nearly trapped by tidal inlets, and ended up detouring inland and skipping over a railway line. Thankfully, we avoided the Fat Controller and his extortionate fixed penalty. All this didn't curb their enthusiasm for praying, and who knows what God thought about it all? That night Chris, along with son Sam and nephew Mike, linked up with us at another bunkhouse. Before setting off, we had a group-cooked brekkie which must have fuelled our spiritual strength.

We had a number of positive encounters including knocking on a stranger's car window and asking if he knew anyone who needed praying for. His somewhat surprising reply was, "Yes, me, please!" His face told the story of a bad week. We prayed there and then and moved on. A few minutes down the road Chris felt led to go back, and give him a card with a Bible verse on it saying, "He heals the brokenhearted, and binds up their wounds."

Walking to Machynlleth was really hard for me. I was so sick that eating wasn't a possibility. Having used up just about the last reserves of strength, I was running on empty. It is weird how lack of physical energy can have a knock-on effect regarding your emotions. I looked like a bag of crap, and felt like it too! But it is often when we are at our lowest that God shows up with an encouragement. I had a great chat with some guy in the pub. Tears filled his eyes, as I shared the story of the prodigal son. It was good to be able to share about God's individual love for him, in spite of the fact that I wasn't feeling that love for myself at the time.

Aberystwyth, Aberaeron, Cardigan, Fishguard = 76 miles

Watching Tom happily tuck into a hearty lunch made my stomach churn, and I even had to put up with him rubbing my nose in it. It was not the only time that God pre-arranged someone from home to be alongside me in a moment of particular need. Thanks, mate! Every third weekend I had an extra free day. Was it only a coincidence that it had been scheduled in the midst of that personal storm? The weight of the rucksack had become intolerable: it felt more like carrying a juggernaut! From a little nipper I have adored that pink, banana-flavoured medicine. Now, once again, I had a supply, along with one of those fantastic, clear plastic spoons which make all the difference. A special mention needs to be made of the amazing care and dedication shown by the Cartlidge family.

During this period, I was under more than one kind of attack, and several times temptation painted enticing pictures of the comforts of home. I'd even started to receive some death threats that were coming through to my mobile, which were quite specific and scary. But in the middle of everything that was going on, I had never felt so close to God in all my life. Those verses that come from Isaiah that talk about the fact that even young people get tired and faint, but strength comes to those that wait on the Lord kept me going – as well as the age-old song from primary school – "He's Got the Whole World in His Hands".

Jackie runs a furniture shop project, where old cast-off furniture is restored and sold cheapily to needy families. When she heard the doctor's diagnosis that I had got food poisoning, I guess you could say she treated me as part of the furniture and she and a friend anointed me with oil and prayed for my healing. Strength seemed to come to me immediately.

St David's, Broadhaven, Millford Haven, Tenby = 56 miles

Have you ever thought, "If this wind blows any harder I may well lift off the ground, and start flying"? Luckily it was behind me as I tornadoed along to St David's. My spirit was as uplifted as my body, due to some incredible recent answers to prayer. It was all topped off as I went to evensong at the Cathedral. Generally I'm not into choirs, but this was special. I found myself weeping as they sang, "The Lord is my Shepherd".

I had some extra mileage to cover somehow, to reach hosts well inland. As I queued in the local co-op and asked about bus times, lo and behold the person behind me was going to the same destination, and even knew my host's address.

I spent a day praying at Bongo Clive's Rhythm Shack. He, Julie and Gemma have a vision to reach the lost through music and a café they are setting up. Clive is heavily involved with kids' parties, schools, mental hospitals, prisons, events, everything! I had the chance to go to one of his Kids' Parties, and help set up all his rhythmic gear. Then I sat back to enjoy the do. It was class to be able to witness freely to the birthday girl's dad, which was made easy because of the foundation Clive had laid.

Staying at the Rhythm Shack was a pure delight. The local Baptist Church now has more children and young people than adults, partly because of Bongo and his God. It is a good job that Baptists go for the complete cold dunk, because we got fully immersed just standing watching their fireworks display. Talk about the second baptism, it was definitely more than a mere sprinkling as the rain lashed down yet again.

I'm afraid that I disappointed Frank and Scilla in Tenby, by failing to act on their suggestion of energizing myself with carrot juice. One man's meat is another man's poison! Lucky I got away with that one ... Hopefully, guzzling some of that rust juice won't be a condition of being invited back sometime.

Laugharne, Carmarthen, Llanelli, Port Eynon = 75 miles

The route to Laughame was more like a paddy field than a footpath. As I attempted to walk under a viaduct, on my way to Kilgetty for a lunch meet-up with Vincent, I suddenly found myself knee deep in manky water. It became obvious that, if I wanted to continue walking forward, a snorkel would shortly become a necessity. A quick check confirmed my worst fears – the support team had neglected to provide me with one! Failing to see ahead, tut, tut! Was it time to think like Hannibal Smith, always ready with a foolproof plan? After much deliberation, I solved it. I turned round! After a two mile detour by road, I found myself at the pub, where the bar staff kindly let me hang out my wet clothes on their radiators, and get changed. It was only right to reward them, so I took the liberty of sharing Jesus. The whole idea of a prayer walk was foreign to the atheist owner, but we had a great chat. It turned out that his wife and son were both Christians, so we ganged up on him!

Before leaving Carmarthen, I shared my story, and answers to prayer, as part of a local radio interview. Outside the station, I met another backpacker, who had already passed me earlier in the day, and we chatted. After he left, I felt that God had more to say to him, and actually prayed for another opportunity to cross his path. Amazingly, having partaken of a scrummy lunch, I suddenly saw him in the distance, walking towards Llanelli. So I slipped on Linford's running slicks, and chased him down.

As I read the *Christian Herald* on my way to Port Eynon, it was encouraging to learn that leaders from one hundred and sixty evangelical churches were currently meeting, to discuss replanting viable churches right across Wales. Talk about being in the right place at the right time!

Swansea, Porthcawl, Cowbridge = 48 miles

I needed to soak in the view from the front patio of Nicholaston House over several hours. It was too good to take in quickly, and I knew the video camera wouldn't do it justice. It was frustrating to know that I was restricted to a few minutes. But Phil and Josh had come to walk and pray, not to gaze at the awe-inspiring views. The incredible scenery didn't stop there at the house either, and thanks to Phil I was able to put a name to the next piece of breathtaking cliff that was about to come our way. It was a bright sunny day, and we found the perfect angle to take pictures of the "three cliffs" – which Phil remembered from his boyhood.

We ended up having a fantastic day together, even though we couldn't find a place to eat lunch, and poor Josh was starving. It was nice to arrive at such considerate hosts as Tim and Ruth, who pandered to my every need. Pub meal, jacuzzi, sauna, a swim, and a DVD. Not bad for Christians!

One fab thing about the walk was that I usually had time to take in what was going on around me, and respond to situations as they arose. There is an old, disabled lady in Porthcawl, who that day had unexpected assistance, as she stood helplessly trying to manoeuvre her crutches, in order to get on her bus home. Everyone else in the queue seemed too busy to notice her dilemma, so I nipped in, and gave her an arm up. I'm not trying to blow my own trumpet here. It's just that sometimes the obvious is in front of us, but we are too busy to notice. On the way to Cowbridge I felt reassured once more that every step of my walk was a prayer, and that's quite a few prayers for this nation. When I arrived, the vicar kindly gave me some money specifically for hiking boots!

Cardiff, Newport, Caldicot, Bristol = 64 miles

It's strange to think that Cardiff was a relatively small town until quite recently. Held by the Romans, 2,000 years ago, it was originally named "Caer Didi" or Fort of Didius (a Roman general). Nowadays it is famous for the Millennium Stadium, which – as a guy with all round sporting interest – is particularly close to my heart. We need a whole lot more sports arenas with retractable roofs all over Britain.

It's easy to look across the Bristol Channel towards the coast of North Devon and West Somerset, and catching a steamer there and back seems to be a totally normal part of everyday life to Cardiffians. If I've got it right, today's successful North Devon tourist industry began when Cardiff grew big, about 150 years ago, and paddle steamers later made it easy for the average Joe to cross the Bristol Channel for a weekend break.

They say that Cardiff is generally drier than much of Wales, and it's true that I enjoyed some better weather whilst in Europe's youngest capital. Maybe not everyone in south Kent knows that Cardiff was only declared capital city of Wales in 1955.

Dreaming of being rich has always appealed to me – for selfless reasons, of course. So it was interesting to know that the third Marquess of Bute, whose father pioneered the flourishing transport industry of coal from the Welsh valleys to the wider world, was deemed in 1866 to be the richest man in the world. I obviously didn't breathe the local air deeply enough whilst passing the Castle where the Bute family lived, since so far there has not been any sudden upsurge in my prospects!

It was John (a council youth worker) who taught me about the rich/poor divide in the city, and opened my eyes concerning how bad it was working with young people in some parts of the city. It dawned on me that by comparison with John I am wrapped in cotton wool when it comes to encountering raw life.

By way of a rare change I made my way to Newport on a cold, crisp morning. You appreciate these days so much more, when most of the time it has been slogging it down. Either God or the sunshine prompted me to say affirming words to random passers-by. Sometimes it works, sometimes I wish I hadn't said anything. Are you ever so captured by a film that you imitate the characters? In the film *Patch Adams* Robin Williams conducts an experiment to test human responses, by doing or saying out-of-the-ordinary things. That day I became Patch Adams, and to judge from the smiles on people's faces I must have got it right. One guy was so pleased that fifteen minutes after we had parted, he turned up again on his bike wanting to know more about me and the walk.

Having heard so much about the view over the Severn Bridge, and listened to conflicting opinions from hosts as to whether pedestrians could actually cross it, it was disappointing to find my whole being enveloped in white mist as I trudged over. I could hardly see my own nose (which according to some mates Pinocchio would be proud of) let alone the must vaunted panoramic views down the Bristol Channel. Still, well done to all those hosts who were right!

I found base at Alastair and Jo's who treated me like a king! Not only did I see my first live rugby match, but I also got to see a memorable result – Bristol beat Sale. As we talked I found out that Alastair had a Lotus Elan, and it was as if he read my thoughts because moments later I was roaring away giving it a Lamb test drive. (If truth be known I bottled it slightly, when it came to putting down the hammer.) And then it was off home for a week's break, courtesy of Mike, and his wannabe hearse!

Great; I had finished Wales with nearly four thousand miles under my belt, and now all that remained was the small matter of the final five hundred and fifty miles, round the South West Peninsula, and homeward along the south coast to Kent.

Weston-Super-Mare, Bridgwater, Watchet, Minehead = 71 miles

As we left Bristol, Vincent and I chose to go over Clifton Suspension Bridge where we stopped and thought about those who had taken their own lives in pursuit of elusive happiness. We prayed against the spirit of suicide which seemed so dominant in that place. Our day plan took us through Wraxall where we heard that in Nailsea, the next village on, suicide had actually won a tragic recent victory over a church leader. We made our way there and prayed with Ken, a close friend of the deceased. Strange, don't you think, how our day started with thinking about suicide, and then ended by dealing with its terrible reality? If only we knew a way of showing people contemplating such an awful solution that God really loves them.

It was becoming my habit by now to try the church door wherever I visited. I generally found them open, and often at least one person was around. Somewhere around the Brean/ Berrow area I found a church caretaker about to finish his hoovering. He was really pleased to see me despite the mound of mud spraying from my boots. We sat and had a long chinwag. Then this legend of a man overlooked both my muddy footprints, and also the trail of breadcrumbs which resulted from munching my lunch in that sacred edifice. But not everyone in the town was pleased to see me, as I discovered later on, when I offended a lady at a bus stop by telling her that God loved her. Every face tells a story, and I knew I had dropped a clanger, so I moved sheepishly on.

In Watchet, feeling uncomfortable because I hadn't talked to many people, I went to the lengths of buying a new tee-shirt, with the sole aim of creating an opportunity for conversation. There's a good excuse for shopping, ladies! The staff in the shop let me pray with them. Well, I suppose that old tee-shirt did need replacing.

As I neared the land of Butlin's I felt the unnecessary urge to have a pint, so I stopped at The Smugglers Pub and snuck in a beer. During my somewhat extended stay I noticed that no-one else had stopped by for a re-fuel. The barman and I must have been nattering uninterrupted for ages. I never thought before that a barman's job could be quite lonely. As usual, the walk was the theme, and he appeared to be impressed.

Anyone who has tried to leg it up Porlock Hill must find it an unforgettable challenge. During an extremely winding ascent of less than three miles you actually climb another 1,350 feet above the level of the Bristol Channel, which stretches scarily but beautifully below. You have to feel sorry for the horses which drudged daily up this particular hill, drawing heavy passenger coaches behind them, a practice which ended less than ninety years ago. It's also fun to imagine the scene, and the driver's emotions in 1900 when, for the sake of a bet, a motor car first successfully scaled the hill and looked across at the wild countryside of nearby Exmoor.

I'm a bit of a fan of thatched cottages, and Porlock has a plentiful choice. Maybe the poet Coleridge was staying in one over two hundred years back when – according to him – he was interrupted by "a person from Porlock" and consequently forgot the main plot of the poem "Kubla Khan" which he was writing. It seems, though, that other people were disinclined to believe him, and accused him of an opium hangover. We shall never know, but Coleridge's story strikes me as being about as bizarre as the claim that William Blake was inspired to write his poem "Jerusalem" by looking across from Porlock at the part of the coastline where Jesus (according to legend) once landed to pay a visit to St Joseph of Arimathea. Apparently Joseph was living in the area at the time.

But at least Porlock has more than its fair share of local folklore and tradition, and throughout the walk it was always good to come across places like this, full of character and history.

Lynton, Ilfracombe, Braunton, Westward Ho! = 58 miles

It takes someone like Peter Hall (the Church's Paula Radcliffe) to choose what are claimed to be some of the steepest hills in England to test his resolve. That whole day would be spent climbing steep hill after steep hill. At a moment when I myself was feeling totally knackered, having reached the very top of about our fifth hill, Paula (I mean Peter) decided to let his hair down, and peg it into the next valley, leaving me trailing in his wake.

My host Graham is part of an amazing initiative which is based in Barnstaple. It is called the Freedom Centre, and provides a range of services to members of the community who are experiencing difficulties in their lives. This project reaches out to the homeless, and to people with substance-use problems, mental health issues, backgrounds of offending behaviour or other life-controlling addictions. The Centre provides a drop-in area, six-week healthy eating programme, free gym, computer suite, training room and semi-supported housing for men in recovery from substance use. Since its 2003 beginnings, when a monthly total of two hundred and thirty eight people were dropping in, numbers have increased to an average of over one thousand over the same period.

On the way from Ilfracombe to Braunton I went for a change of approach – reading and walking, and waiting for others to talk to me. It worked. The rucksack seemed to change from being a bit of a burden into a conversational aid. A fella that was loading his car with tools reckoned he had never previously met someone who could walk and read at the same time. He listened to me, and then asked for prayer for one of his colleagues. Reading and walking did occasionally make me a bit disorientated, and this led to some interesting interaction with a lady who had every reason to believe that I was going to walk into her driveway! I stuck to the same format as I moved on to Westward Ho! An old man watched me taking a photo of some birds, and gave me the benefit of his vast wisdom on the subject, before changing to the subject of my walk and what I was doing.

Hartland Point, Bude, Camelford, Wadebridge = 62 miles

Between Westward Ho! and Hartland Point, I met a couple of very wacky South African hikers who obviously loved getting soaked, and insisted on taking my photo, because they were convinced that I would become famous. Not long after this, I felt the tug of my Achilles tendon, which brought back memories of my second trial walk. Was this going to bring the walk to a premature end? I dragged myself to some cover under a bus shelter, and rang Vincent. He had already been prompted to make his way over from Kent by some inner urgency which he didn't understand himself. He caught up with me and we cheated the last few miles by driving to Hartland Quay hotel, where I dived straight for the bath, desperate to ease the pain. Next day we headed immediately for Barnstaple casualty unit, where I was given pain killers, and a scary threat – the problem would either clear up within twenty-four hours, or the show was over. So I gave it a day's rest, and we opted instead for dropping into various churches between Hartland and Bude, in order to stay on schedule.

Phew! When I awoke the following morning I felt fit and ready for the walk to Camelford. We made it, and spent some time in the local New Age shop where the duty manager was more than ready to have a chat. We nattered away for about half an hour – she believed in a higher spiritual awareness, and was simply disillusioned with church. Unfortunately, we couldn't argue with what she said about her personal experiences as she clearly wasn't cared for. But we could present God differently from how she understood Him, and Vincent made a point of writing to her when he got back to Kent.

I prayed as I woke Sunday morning in Wadebridge that God would arrange for a first timer to come to church. So it was with a burst of inner excitement that I heard the pastor mention, unprovoked, that he had indeed noticed a new visitor as he gazed around the meeting. The sense of God being at work behind the scenes continued in the evening meeting as a quote was read out of the very same book I was reading at the time – the exact page I had reached – cool!

Newquay and the Isles of Scilly = 16 miles

I can see why sixth-formers gather here to celebrate the end of their exams. The beach is vast, the waves massive, and all of it is just a stone's throw away from the town with its string of pubs and clubs. It is no surprise that the population swells from around twenty thousand to over one hundred thousand in the summer. It suddenly dawned on me how much I liked this remote shoreline walking in the crisp winter months with few people about. It had more appeal than summer beaches

overcrowded with people and littered with discarded newspapers and half-eaten ice creams, to say nothing of the manky
unmentionables! Of course, the visual downside was that,
instead of relishing the sight of bikini-clad beauties, all I had to
admire were my own footprints mapping a solitary path
across the smooth, golden sand. (Cue the violins...)

A trip to the wonderful Scilly Isles would have been
unlikely on my budget – and also unthought of – but for
the slick awareness of the support team, and the extreme
generosity of two individuals. Without any effort on my part,
I found myself boarding an early twelve-seater flight to
St Mary's on 13th December.

Poor old Sir Cloudesley Shovell. Not only did he have to
live with a name like that, but he was the guy in charge of the
British fleet which sank off the Scilly Isles in 1707. A simple
navigational error drove all his ships onto the dangerous local
rocks. The catastrophe, which took the lives of over 1,500
sailors, is still considered one of the worst disasters in British
naval history. Soon after my walk finished, a team from
Bristol University began a study of one of the wrecks, *HMS
Firebrand*. It's funny to think that the English were so
successful at scattering hostile fleets by sending fireships in
amongst them, and that *Firebrand*'s mere presence would
have spread fear in the enemy ranks, whereas now she lies
rotting on the Atlantic seabed. I'm not so great with
orienteering myself, apart from my Satnav. But it's easy to
understand why this mishap forced the British government
to get going with finding a more reliable way to define
longitude. If there had been one before, Sir Cloudesley and his
fleet would have arrived safely back at port.

Doing the walk brought out in me quite an enthusiasm for
noticing birds (yes – the feathered variety), and the Scilly Isles
are particularly good for this, since they are a bit of a welcome
stop-off point for weary wings. Doing just a day visit restricted
me to the main island only – St Mary's, where all the

passenger flights and mainland ferries arrive. I'm told that wreck-diving is a very popular organized activity, and it would have been good to see a few of the many seals which are said to inhabit some of the smaller spots.

Visiting the Scilly Islands on a day flight from Newquay made me feel slightly disorientated – I still had a long way to actually walk to Land's End, but here I was, just twenty-eight miles west of that famous place, and I would have to head north-east again in order to cover the ground properly.

You can't really talk about Scilly without learning the word "archipelago". My problem is that – as soon as I learn it – my forgettory clicks in again! Anyway, that is the word used to describe a group of islands in a large body of water, so I must try to remember it, and it certainly fits the fifty-five islands and over ninety rocks which make up the Scillies. The name was originally "Sully", which I believe means "The Sun Isles", and local weather records prove that the area really does have a very high proportion of sunshine. It was good to learn that John Wesley took the trouble to visit the islands and preach the gospel. He also founded a number of chapels, though it was a bit disappointing to discover that a tourist centre is now based in one of these, sadly no longer required for its original purpose of worshipping God.

Winter visitors seemed to provoke suspicion amongst some of the locals. I got a strong sense of being an intruder in a close-knit community. There was time to visit a number of pubs and cafés, where usually my rucksack would have been enough to stimulate curiosity. It proved not to be the case in St Mary's. It was always me who started any conversation, and that was brief, apart from two friendly old ladies who I got the impression were visitors anyway. In general, although there was friendly chatter going on all around me, I was aware of being on the outside, slightly jealous of their relaxed togetherness. I never did really get to find out about the people of Scilly. Who were they? Did they

work? What brought them there? Did they get to experience
life beyond their locality? Flying back I felt I had visited the
island, but not its inhabitants.

Camborne, St Ives, Sennen (Land's End) = 41 miles

Ambling towards Camborne I decided it was a day for
dropping in at pubs. I called for a pint and lunch at Peterville
pub in St Agnes' village, and enjoyed an interesting chat with
the staff there.

We shared opinions about how important it was for the
church to be involved in the community, and especially about
how pastors, vicars and the like need to get down to the local
pubs. They were full of praise for their local pastor, and how
relational he was. It's not often I go in to a pub and hear
churches being "bigged-up". It was a refreshing change. So,
whoever the minister is, "Well done for making a difference!"

Next I popped in to the Old School pub at St Hawke. Cool!
A couple of the locals and I enjoyed a drink together.

Having left website cards at both pubs I felt I had done the
job, as it were. It would be nice to hear from you, if you ever
read this book.

You have to get there early in the winter if you want to
make the best of Land's End.

It turned out that there was an exhibition centre for people
who had completed the epic journey from John O'Groats to
Land's End which advertised a video showing all the weird and
wonderful ways in which people have covered the distance. It
would have been good to learn more about the guy who
actually did it on stilts, or the other fella who preferred a
shopping trolley! Since my walk ended, I hear that Alan raised
over £1,000 for the excellent cause of Breast Cancer Care, by
driving the full eight hundred and seventy four miles in his
Vivaro van, on a single tank of fuel. Nevertheless, on the day
of my visit I was somewhat smugly looking forward to

highlighting the superiority of my own achievement, but I didn't get the chance to gloat, because not much happens there on a cold, dark late afternoon in December. To my severe disappointment, everything was completely closed. Presumably my home support team had forgotten to advise the local authorities that one of an elite band of pedestrian coastal circumnavigators was planning to bestow on them the majestic honour of his presence that day.

If you have graced both ends of our land I'm sure you would agree that John O'Groats has a bit of work to do if it wants to be more of a tourist magnet, whereas Land's End has at least made a start. As I rounded the south western tip of Britain, a surge of anticipation welled up at the thought of having finally entered the home straight of my marathon.

Penzance, Helston, Coverack, Falmouth = 58 miles

As everyone knows, when you have a haircut either you are stuck with the barber gabbing on, or vice versa. That lady in Helston not only found herself faced with shearing my extremely windswept mop, but also having to come to terms with my endless nattering! After doing so much listening for months on end, I was determined to get in first with my topic of conversation. She loved it though, and was totally enthralled by the adventure. Unfortunately, she wasn't too interested in the Christian aspect of the journey. But, hey, you never know!

The Sunday before Christmas the children stole the show at John and Caroline's church – it was nativity day. That would have tired most people out but – although Caroline was ridden with cancer – she made a cracking lunch for eight of us. Sundays were a family day, so it was a privilege to be invited in. No TV, but the sweets come in, and the games come out. Everyone really looks forward to it. *Taboo* was on the agenda, and for that nothing works better than the grudge match – the

stronger sex vs the weaker (joking, OK?). Final result delayed
pending stewards' enquiry – there are a number of complaints
outstanding!

Dad, Mark and Shane made the long drive down to
Helston. Shane stayed with me for my second night at John
and Caroline's – or rather a nice caravan in the backyard –
while Dad and Mark enjoyed their five-star luxury holiday
mansion, before linking up with us for a two day trail around
the Lizard. All three took turns at either walking with me, or
driving on ahead, so that we could keep Dad's car close by all
the time. Old boy (Chopper Lamb) was first up as we trekked
past Mullion down towards Lizard Point. Dad distinctly
remembers having to dodge large numbers of rather mean
looking bulls. In fact, he got so freaked out thinking that one
was eyeballing him that we had to make at least a mile detour
round the back of them.

We met the lads at Polbream Cove and not-so-little Lamb
took up the baton. We had walked barely a few miles when he
complained of calf strain climbing up a hefty piece of cliff
incline. I caught up with all the youth work he had been doing
in our local church, including his latest idea to start up a
"youth church". We finally met the other two for a spot of
late lunch, and beers!

Then Shane joined me for the final leg. We saw some
absolutely amazing scenery as we passed Black Head on our
way to Coverack. Shane could hardly believe his eyes, having
only been used to all that Folkestone seafront had to offer. We
must have been appreciating the views a bit too much,
though, because we were well out on our timings. It started
to get dark, and slippery. Walking the coastal path was far too
risky, so we had to venture inland and cut across some old
unkempt fields. We ended up stepping in numerous deep
muddy puddles. To add to our woes, it started chucking it
down. I knew that Dad would be worrying, so we had to
break into a full-on attempted sprint (not easy with a rucksack

stuck to your back) for as long as we could . . . We made it, but very late!

After a final night enjoying the comforts of the Angel Hotel, and a rare win over my brother at pool, we headed home for Christmas to meet Santa.

> "It was as I pulled my overworked calf, dragging myself up yet another steep hill, that I thought, 'rather him than me!'"
> **Mark** *(brother)*
>
> "What an experience, the walk was amazing! God walked every step, and so did we!"
> ***Shane***

Truro, Saint Austell, Lostwithiel, Liskeard = 45 miles

Christmas, as usual, was a real blast. In amongst my bulging sack of socks and deodorant was some money Santa left me for a guitar. Maybe he thought that the one way to fund the rest of my journey might be to take up busking? Obviously no-one had told him about my squeaky vocal chords.

Sam sacrificed the pleasures of studying for his finals in architecture and escaped the frantic last-minute preparations for his (*July!*) wedding . . . I was of course already finalising my best man's speech. Dig complete, or is it? Having made the trip back to Falmouth in his rust bucket, I was ready to believe that the next day's walk to Truro would be a quicker option.

Most of our day was spent catching up with each other, and discussing in some depth our responsibility when it comes to witnessing to our families and friends. We got a bit tangled up trying to decide what the Bible teaches in terms of which is the more populated – heaven or hell? Then, just to simplify matters, we moved on to defining whether or not – if hell is

The May boys getting ready to help me capture Dover Castle

Cheesey or what!

I made it – it's all downhill from here

Sleeping on the job

Preparing my next sermon at Portland Bill

Dymchurch Ken – eight years short of a ton!

The tide can be dangerous at Three Cliffs Bay, The Gower

Anyone see the Severn Bridge?

Certainly wouldn't be my last beer though

Looking forward to the four hundred mile sprint finish

Legend has it that giants built St Michael's Mount

It gets hairier further on

fuller – the devil has any scope to claim a small victory in the midst of crushing defeat. Please refer to the theological greats on this one! Or come back to me in fifty years time. I wonder if I will have an answer even then! Sam at any rate went back home with plenty to think about, and I'd really enjoyed the company of one of my best mates.

Having reached Lostwithiel a bit early I stopped of in a small busy café. God had planted a couple of Christians who kept asking all the right questions while everyone else was listening.

"For Ron and myself at Hartswell Farm, it was a real blessing to spend time with Gary and the others who shared that evening. Since their visit, there has been a stirring-up in Lostwithiel, to go deeper, for many, and to wrestle in prayer particularly for those who are sick, and there is an expectation for God to be glorified in signs and wonders. For me, the memory of walking the first mile uphill out of Lostwithiel, and trying to keep up with you, was personally special. On the return journey, my feet never touched the ground!"

Wendy Jordan (Hartswell Farm)

The coastal route then took me on to Looe, where I met Steve in a pub. For the last three years he has been walking on and off, sleeping rough, in shelters, or occasionally in churches. He believed that God sent him on a mission to leave poems in churches, reminding people that we are living in the last days. We walked four miles and prayed together. It was a good time, and we parted as friends that day. I found the church in Liskeard very warm and welcoming. Although it was a small set-up, many of the congregation came and spoke to me.

Plymouth, Ivybridge, Salcombe, Dartmouth = 66 miles

Making tracks towards Torpoint, I had another really positive feedback about Christians. A guy in a pub admitted that during his life he has rarely spoken to strangers, or offered help to someone in obvious need. His priority has been to look after number one. However, he remembers earlier times of need in his own life, including homelessness. But on each occasion it was always a Christian who helped him. Each smile, every meaningful conversation – it was a Christian. They seemed different, not in it solely for themselves.

Ralph (my host) accompanied me as we boarded a highly efficient chain-operated ferry, saying goodbye to yet another county as we left Cornwall and re-entered Devon.

It was back to the hustle and bustle of civilization and swarms of people, rushing around – going nowhere fast. Plymouth certainly has enough of a past to satisfy a much keener historian than myself. You could drown yourself in the tidal wave of information about the city's life. Six hundred years ago it was actually burnt by the French, but had recovered well by the reign of the first Queen Elizabeth, just two centuries later. Speaking of that queen, it's a bit of a shock to find that she sponsored some of her Plymouth-based fleet to capture slaves from West Africa to work in the Americas.

Pocahontas, the beautiful native American princess, landed here in 1616, and four years later the famous *Mayflower* voyage sailed out, bearing the group who were to become known as the "Pilgrim Fathers" of the USA. Not so many people, perhaps, know that the emperor Napoleon was imprisoned here for two weeks, before going into permanent exile on St Helena, or that – almost a century later – the few survivors of the crew of the wrecked *Titanic* found their way here first.

It's nearly two hundred years since the strongest recorded tornado in the UK struck Plymouth. During World War II the town was massively blitzed – as the Nazis sought to destroy one of the chief British naval dockyards. I definitely hadn't previously known before just how bad things were at that time, to the point where the pre-war population of over 220,000 was almost halved at one stage. How inspiring, though, to learn a bit more about the nature of the resistance of those being so severely attacked. While everything was being blown to bits, someone set up a simple wooden sign over the door of St Andrew's church, with one Latin word on it – *Resurgam*, which (I'm told) means "I shall rise again". It reminds me of the sort of things Jesus was saying to His friends, as He saw His death getting nearer, and His promise was the same – "I shall rise again!"

Hopefully, the Christians in Plymouth will receive the same message today, from the same risen Christ, and be greatly encouraged to soldier on.

It was hard to take in everything Ralph was saying, Plymouth has got such a rich history. But, to be honest, I had become more accustomed to the slower pace of life, and although my body was in Plymouth, my mind was with the people of Cornwall. I'm not much of a big city person, so it was good to see things calm down a bit as I headed towards Ivybridge, the gateway to South Dartmoor. The bridge itself crossed the river Erme, and was appropriately clothed with tangled ivy bearing the green berries of winter. Next day, it was up the steep hill into Salcombe, the southernmost town in the South Hands. The main town is squeezed against the seafront, backed by an increasingly steep green incline and built around Kingsbridge estuary. The mild climate supports palms as high as Bolt Head, from which unbelievable views are there for free.

There was another newcomer at John and Val's weekly house meeting in Dartmouth. He was a boyfriend of one of the ladies there. Later on, I found out that he was struggling with life in general, and especially with having recently been made redundant. Very frustrated and amazingly honest – a refreshing combination! I had a little slot given over to talking about the ups and downs of walking around Britain's coast-line. As I shared about my own experiences with the same kind of brutal honesty, I could see his heart warming again towards the God he had been disconnected from for quite a while. He walked out a different man – I think.

Torquay, Newton Abbot, Exeter = 33 miles

On the way to Torquay, John Fudge and I spent ages looking for the long-lost answer to finding heaven. And yes we did finally stumble upon that blasted fish and chip shop! We had our fill, only to find that our eyes had been too big for our bellies – talk about that after lunch feeling. We dawdled along after that for quite some time. I find that we stir each other up spiritually. Both of us want to see so much more of God in our nation, and the lives of the young people we are in contact with. After a good chat with a postman named John, we offered him prayer, and he snapped it up. His dad had cancer, so please join our prayers for a miracle for him, even now. As was becoming customary we prayed there and then on the street. He was also so pleased to receive a tract about finding Jesus, and asked quite innocently whether he would be allowed keep it. Wonderful moment! We handed another few tracts out throughout the day, and prayed for Crusaders (a youth organization that John works for). A friend of John's phoned, so we prayed for him too.

Just as it appeared that the day was winding up, it all seemed to start. We had a good twenty-minute chat with a group of what the world would call "no hopers". This was a bit nerve-racking to begin with, but we got into it, and they really respected us for our bravery in confronting them. We left them with the challenge to check out their local church, and give God a try. Who knows?

No sooner had my good friend Fudgey boy left, than another close mate – Tom – arrived, and we checked in together at Rora House. It felt good to be there with Malcolm and Christine, because it reminded me of our shared interest in Romania. Rora House partners up with Aurora Christian Association, and owns a great place in Brasov where I have often been part of a team doing ministry and humanitarian work.

We started the next day off on the right foot, with an early morning prayer meeting with Malcolm and Christine and set off for Exeter. First up, we climbed to the top of a hill, and prayed for our nation. There was a bright shining light across the sea, which helped us pray about the light of God. That day every person we stopped and chatted to was a Christian. Do you know what? There are more out there than you think, so be encouraged! We had a really good conversation with Rob and Ivor. One had cancer, the other was recovering from a quad heart bypass. You might think that they had every reason to grumble, but they are two of the most joyful Christians I've met. We also decided to interview a random couple on the video camera. They were fine with it. They called themselves Christians, but they weren't sure about needing to be born again. Unfortunately, we didn't have time to go into it, as they found a convenient moment to slip away. Tom and I summoned up enough energy from somewhere to go to an evening prayer meeting. We weren't disappointed, as God really moved our hearts.

Exmouth, Seaton, Bridport, Weymouth = 71 miles

Tom and I stopped for an early lunch before he was due to catch a train back from Exton to his car. A coal fire blazed invitingly, as we exchanged niceties with the barman, who was so interested in the walk that he shouted us our beers for free, unusual for England – Scotland had the upper hand on that front. By the time we left, it seemed that everyone who worked in the pub knew my name, and what I was about. My time with Tom was class, and I prayed that its impact would remain with him.

Even though I had only met Andy and Jenny the once, from one of my trial walks, their home was familiar enough for me to settle in easily, and we carried on effortlessly from where we had left off eighteen months previously. Great couple! The coastal path to Seaton was inspiring, but steep. Walking was hard work that day, but it didn't stop me from singing, or my camera from snapping. The Christian retreat centre at Upcot was an obvious place for me to stay overnight, the staff were really funny and welcoming, and I fitted in straight away. I left as the pool champ!

People from back home kept phoning to warn me of potential danger, having heard about the serious cliff falls at Charmouth days before my arrival. I stopped for a rest in Lyme Regis, and was slightly disappointed to find the views obstructed by sea defence construction work, so I sat down on a seafront bench and buried my head in the newspaper. The old lady sitting nearby was easy to talk to and showed enthusiasm about the walk. Before I could get round to mentioning its Christian aspect, she stood up, and – placing her hand on my head – blessed me with the words "The Lord will reward you". That was a bit of a spooky gob-smacker, and left me mystified, but uplifted.

Having finished the day's section early a hair chop beckoned, but no barber's shop could be found. As usual there was a reason – God meant me to keep looking until I found someone who was on His agenda. The lady who ended up cutting my hair was ready to talk about her loneliness and the feeling that it would be good to try church some-time. You can guess what I said! I didn't always score too highly in observation tests, so it came as no surprise to see how many barbers' shops I had missed on the way. Maybe God had allowed my weakness to be woven into His plan that day?

Our ex multi-marathon church bigwig and his adorable wife met up with me in Bridport for the day's stretch towards Weymouth. It was a real honour to walk first with Graham, and then with Deirdre. What struck me most about my time with Graham was his humility and honesty. The baton was then passed to Deirdre for the last few miles before a welcome lunch. Her compassionate praying is always touching and inspirational.

Portland Bill, Swanage, Poole, Lymington = 88 miles

It was a bleak, cold, windy afternoon as we neared Portland Bill. On our way, after having climbed a mammoth hill, Vincent and I came across an observatory, where volunteer staff monitor the safety of the shipping lanes in the Channel. Off the cuff, we cheekily started climbing the access stairs to see who was about. The guys on duty made us very welcome, and explained how the system worked. There were gadgets everywhere, and the views weren't half bad either! It wasn't long before the topic of conversation swung round from them to us, and what on earth we were doing pleasure walking on a day like that. Moments later we were praying for healing in their friends' lives.

In an area which appeared to be run down, and in a state of hopelessness, we stumbled across an unexpected treasure. As usual, we popped into a church purely because it was open, and found a small children's club in progress, under the leadership of a deaconess, who we fondly remember as the "booster lady". So far as could be told she made it her life's business to affirm everyone she met.

Durdle Door was a sight to behold, watching aggressive waves smash their way through the eroding defences of the grey-white rock stack, as they have been doing for centuries, enlarging the rugged archways which in years to come will doubtless expand into open gaps. To the west, we strolled – or rather staggered – up Swyre Head, where we had a discussion about how (in my opinion) the fresh coastal air I had been inhaling for the last nine months seemed to have immunized me from the common cold. Vincent rather spiritually suggested there might well be a connection between other people's prayers and my good health! Right then a lady came puffing up the steep slope – as we listened to her, we discovered that she was under doctor's orders to get some fresh air to help combat her bronchitis. There was no way, coming immediately from a debate on prayer, to ignore the fact that this was God's timing.

Brenda gave me much more than a nice meal, and a warm bed to sleep in. This amazing lady also rolled up her sleeves, and got stuck into a morning's walk between Poole and Lymington. Our prayer agenda covered local schools particularly, before she left me to mull over a prophetic word about being a spiritual dad to lots of children. As I walked along the seafront, it was obvious that a lady nearby needed help if she was ever going to get into her beach hut. Not exactly my cup of tea, but opening the outside door of the cabin later allowed me to knock on the inside door of her spiritual life. People don't care how much you know, until they know how much you care.

Yarmouth, Ventnor, Ryde, Cowes, Lymington = 55 miles

After our eventful walk from Yarmouth to Ventnor (described in the appendix) an uplifted Richard took himself back via the ferry to Lymington, and home for a weekend in Kent. But I was not alone for long; one of our church families has relatives on the Isle of Wight, so three of them came down as I continued round the island towards Ryde. Priscilla, Tom and Harry were with me for the whole eighteen mile stretch, which considering Harry was only ten, and as involved as the rest of us were in praying for people, was a quite remarkable feat.

The four of us had a bird-counting competition, which

Tom won hands down. It was quite amazing to watch the black-moustached peregrine falcons hovering motionless above their prey, wings spread and body taut poised for the kill. The most breathtaking part, though, was to see so many of them swoop at incredible speed in pursuit of their quarry. This hunting dive is said by many authorities to make these falcons the fastest creatures on the planet, possibly reaching beyond 200 mph at maximum velocity.

In fact, the island has an incredible variety of birds which we could look out for. These included bluethroats (merely a blue excuse for a robin), hawkfinches (fierce-looking heavy-weight cousins of the green species) and woodcocks, whose rather tubby bodies clash oddly with their long, thin beaks. Presumably two woodcocks who fancied even a little kiss would have to stand on opposite sides of the island!

Priscilla pointed out a guillemot, which was the nearest thing to a penguin that I saw on the entire walk, and it amazes me how the tree sparrow can keep its tail cocked apparently the whole time. You can't help feeling a bit sorry for the common sandpiper, whose vocal range is seemingly limited to just three notes and who has to fly from the south to the north at breeding time.

But it wasn't all play, as we focused on what we were really there to do, making contact with people from all walks of life. One lady was feeling particularly low, being unwell herself and having to get ready to send her dog in for an operation. Her emotions were unconcealed, as she responded gratefully to Priscilla's prayers. In fact, I was maybe the least successful walker of the day, since when I went to shake hands with a caretaker of another church he was blatantly scared, and kept backing away from me. As we left, feeling rather uncomfortable, he could be seen following from a distance until we were well clear.

Priscilla's parents did a fantastic job of looking after us all, and made sure I was introduced to their vicar who gave me freedom to share at the church. I now know that what I had to say made a specific difference to one particular person, who consequently decided to be baptised. Not for the first time, I was struck by the humility of a church leader, as the vicar sought my advice regarding youth and children's work.

> "Every day each one of us has the potential to make an impact on the lives of people we meet and speak to, if we are open to the Holy Spirit guiding us."
>
> **Priscilla**
>
> "The greatest thing about walking with Gary was seeing his devotion and commitment towards God."
>
> **Harry**
>
> "Gary's prayer walk brought people together while supporting him. The amount of prayer he received was huge!"
>
> **Tom**

It was impossible to be in Cowes for very long, without noticing how many up-and-coming events were being publicized. I don't suppose there are many places that offer more by way of sail-power, gentle rally or competitive racing. But I had to move on; no time to mooch around and watch the many boats bouncing gently on their moorings.

The ferry bore me safely back to Lymington, where I was welcomed once more by Phil and Heather. They had kindly laid on a spread at their home for me and whoever wanted to come. About ten of us tucked in heartily and talked into the night. No agenda, just family being together.

Southampton, Portsmouth, Chichester, Bognor Regis = 62 miles

Mike made his fourth (and by now considerably shorter) journey to meet me for lunch, and this time added in a trip to a motor museum. We really enjoyed this sneak insight into what life was like back in the old days, and how much time people had for each other. Later on, Mike happened to mention the story of ten lepers being healed, but nine not bothering to come back to say "thank you". How about that? The previous few days I had been thinking about that very story, and my need to thank God for what He does for me. We did some walking, prayed in churches against dodgy stuff in the area, focused on the lonely and reached out to God together for them. One really impressive church had a book you could sign at the back next to a map. You signed your name under a country heading. They had so many countries of the world represented at the church.

> "I found the experience 'umbling, the meals at pubs appropriate and conducive to my constitution, the old cars drool-making and interesting."
>
> **Mike H**

No doubt, if one chooses to walk around the British coastline, an inevitable consequence will be to come across a large number of towns whose history is basically all bound up with the sea. This was especially true of Portsmouth, which still houses the world's oldest dry-dock. Trying to decide exactly how old a town might be isn't exactly my scene, particularly when the theories so far include a date of AD 501 with the founding of the town by a man called Port (!) right through to 1194, when Richard the Lionheart presented the town with its first charter. It is maybe reasonable to agree with those who suspect that the generous reaffirming of this charter by successive kings and queens had something to do with them knowing that Portsmouth was an ideal starting point for anyone wanting to invade France by sea. By all accounts, the town paid a heavy price anyway, being burnt by

French attackers four times during a fifty year period of the fourteenth century, in addition to enduring a devastating outbreak of the plague known as the Black Death.

Unfortunately, before my arrival, the authorities had already completed the demolition of the city's Tricorn Centre, which some people had called the ugliest building in the UK. It would have been good to compare it with some others I saw on my way round the coastline. Instead, the year in which my walk started saw the completion of Portsmouth's wonderful new Spinnaker Tower, near the shoreline. It was probably wise not to join all the tourists who overcame fear of height in order to reach the high observation deck at the top of the tower, from which you can see the whole city as well as the harbour. But, thinking things over, perhaps it would have been good to check out major events in order to time my journey appropriately. For example, I didn't get to Portsmouth until February 2006, eight months after Sea Britain, the town's wonderful spectacular celebration of the two hundredth anniversary of the Battle of Trafalgar. Now that is one small piece of history I actually had heard about before!

The world does not seem to be too full of Portsmouth supporters, but my friend Alex, who is in his eighties, has never stopped banging their drum, and perhaps I should have got myself to Fratton Park just for his sake. But then, my walk never actually took me into Anfield, despite Mark's best efforts!

As Gareth (my Southampton host) and I ventured on towards Portsmouth, the realization of being so near to home suddenly hit me. This was it, in less than two weeks I would be with family and friends, sitting down all day if I wanted to, and lapping up all the praise for a mammoth journey.

I had been to Portsmouth many times before by car from Hythe, and it wasn't that far, not really. As we looked out across our land, we could see plenty to pray for – schools, pubs, churches, and people that went flashing past in cars on their way to who knows where. To our left, Netley Abbey provided an architectural feast for the eyes, one which my buddy Sam would have gobbled up with relish. It seems a shame that Peter des Roches, the thirteenth-century bishop who dreamed up the plans for this fantastic edifice, died well before its completion, leaving it to Henry III to finish the job, and claim all the credit – typical of a king!

It was nice to arrive at Barney's student pad, I didn't know what to expect, but when I saw the string of ladies living there, I knew he hadn't changed much. One of the bonuses of taking up dance for your degree, I suppose. (Billy Elliott, eat your heart out!) That night Barney and his ladies took me to see a dance show. I actually quite liked it, even though Barney thought it was rubbish. Sorry mate, I won't be taking up dance, though! On the way to Bognor, yet another one of Barney's girlfriends (Anna) joined up with his dad, Josh, and me. The Baptist church opposite Barney's house was locked, but we managed to catch Roger's attention through the window, and had a prayer time together. His church is bursting at the seams with young people, and was ready to start Alpha in the workplace.

An art class was going on at St Paul's Church. We invited ourselves in for a cuppa, and prayed with the minister before mingling individually with the artists (about half Christian, half not) I prayed with a lady who had recently lost her husband. She was very grateful and tearful. Josh noticed a man sitting on his own alone outside, so we asked him if he was OK. He said; "No", and told us he had recently split from his wife, and his daughter had an eating disorder. We prayed with him. Finally, we met John, a minister who invited us in for yet another cuppa (tasty!) He was a fantastically humble guy, desperate for his church to revive, and willing to ask strangers like us for advice. It turned out that Barney and Anna might be able to help with some of the church's worship. I was really encouraged to have those three mates with me that day, and later on I was to hear how they felt about it.

> "What most amazed me on my walk with Gary was how much he had grown – not just in his waistline, but in God – and how he so naturally got alongside people and shared Jesus with them. God bless you, Gary"
>
> **Stephen**
>
> "Walking with Gary gave me a greater passion for my uni home, Chichester. Also, seeing God's work being done in the places where your own faith and courage was tested was a real testimony to Gary's work around Britain ... What an awesome experience!"
>
> **Barney**
>
> "Walking with G was a good eye opener. I got to taste in just two days the power of what he was experiencing throughout the past year."
>
> **Josh**

Littlehampton, Brighton, Eastbourne, Bexhill = 67 miles

As I left the sumptuous en-suite accommodation in Bognor Royal Norfolk Hotel, funded by the Vineyard fellowship, meals and all, it once again made me think, (without being too bigheaded) that Christians really are different. How many people do you know who would provide a complete stranger with luxury, rather than basic hospitality? At long last, Dr Jeremy Russell BSc PhD (aspiring OBE, Nobel prize winner, possibly PM?) managed to pull himself away from clinching another multi-million pound deal, and joined the humble rambler. Did he just happen to select an eight mile stroll on the south coast, as opposed to a twenty mile climb up the west coast of Scotland? I am not sure about this, but I am certain that Jeremy came intending to get stuck in to praying, and he did.

Two of my best mates, Mev and Shane, met up with me on what was to be my last Sunday.

So we hit the Little Hamp Town, and found a pub. Some drunkard stood next to me, propped up at the bar, and started causing a scene. He was right in my face, wanting a fight. So I followed what has become my somewhat shameful habit, and tried to hide behind Mike, who was not happy to say the least, but hard enough to handle it. I felt uneasy, so each of us drank only half of a well deserved beer and moved on.

The sandy beach between Littlehampton and Brighton was dotted with patches of deep water. The challenge of finding the right way to cross each one was a good laugh. We did everything from seeing who could kick pebbles the highest, to talking about everything that life chucks our way, and how we deal with it. I feel it absolutely necessary to mention poor Mev and his bum-chafing, and how slowly we all had to walk.

> " 'For I have the desire to do what is good, but I cannot carry it out. For what I do is not the good I want to do' (Romans 7:18–19). Gary 'did the good' that he wanted to do!"
>
> **Mike**

Each of the Seven Sisters between Brighton and Eastbourne took its own toll of legs and back, as Simon and I struggled against the howling coastal gale. Ahead of us we could see an obscene practical joke. It was a large penis crafted in lumps of limestone – nice one lads – not! We felt stirred to change the sculpture into something more directly worshipful – we chose the words "God loves!".

> "If we weren't praying for or with someone, we continued in good and challenging conversation throughout the day."
>
> **Simon**

Most people have heard of Beachy Head, the notorious cliff close by Eastbourne. When my Rwandan friend, Charles Semwaga, came to Bible College in the UK for a year, he was shocked to hear about this place where so many have taken their own lives, and paid a special visit to pray against the spirit of suicide. May God hear his prayers, and answer them. Perhaps we are too used to the stories, and need to stir up our own spirits to pray also.

By the time of arriving at Eastbourne, my legs were once again aching from walking a succession of steep cliffs where the South Downs meet the sea. Unlike so many of the towns on the walk, Eastbourne is very young, having grown from more or less nothing less than two hundred years ago, as seaside holidays became the fashion. It does appear in the 1086 *Domesday Book*, but only became famous almost 700 years later, when some of George III's children went there for a holiday. The surviving Martello towers, built in the time of Napoleon as a defence against French attack, reminded me of home, where I see several almost every day. But the present town was really just four small villages until 1849, when the arrival of the Brighton and South Coast Railway opened it up to visitors on a huge scale, and brought prosperity to the new town, which the Duke of Devonshire ordered to be "a town built by gentlemen for gentlemen". It's hard to believe that – just over a century and a half ago – records show the population as less than 4,000. However, over the next forty years it grew to above 34,000.

From time to time, I've wondered how I would have coped as a child, sent away from home during World War II. For children connected with Eastbourne, it must have been especially bad. First, the town was used as a base fairly near to London to which evacuees could be sent, but then as things got worse the town itself was seen as dangerous, and children had to be uprooted again and sent further from home and family. To me, that is almost impossible to imagine. But it proved to be a wise precaution, since Eastbourne was to endure more attacks by air than any other town in south-east England.

My own wanderings around the town were rather happier, though it ought to have struck me as odd that so much of the seafront appeared to be occupied by Victorian hotels. Later research explains why – the present Duke of Devonshire still owns these buildings, and is not interested in developing them into shops, so the whole effect is to capture a sense of the past just by walking through, especially as you also go by an old bandstand and pier, which adds to the atmosphere of the past.

For us, the weather was disappointing, and the town didn't live up to what it calls itself in the brochures – "The Sunshine Coast". However, just a couple of years before my visit (July 1911 in fact!) Eastbourne set the all-time record for the highest number of hours of sunshine in a single month – 383.9. Since that represents a daily average of over 12.3 hours, it will presumably take a bit of beating!

Halfway between Eastbourne and Bexhill lies Pevensey Bay, where I met up with Squibbs, Tony, Beryl, Jean and Josie, my young at heart Christian friends from Hythe, whose combined ages totalled three hundred and eighty years.

It was at The Moorings restaurant, right on the stony beach, that we sheltered from the chill factor, despite a blazing sun. Half of us envied the other fifty per cent, as they had the pleasure of a lovely view out of the conservatory window. Together we conquered a sizeable feast, a more acceptable battle than the one between William of Normandy and King Harold on the same site some 949 years earlier. Anyway, Squibbs obviously enjoyed it.

"Taking part in Gary's God-given vision was awe-inspiring, one of the most exciting things I have ever done!"
Josie Thomson

"Gary, to share in your walk, even for such a little way, was a great privilege and pleasure. I was really blessed."

Squibbs Poole

Rye, Lydd, Hythe = 44 miles

One of my most faithful supporters in communication and prayer joined me, as we zeroed in on Rye. Mum and I had an eventful day, which hardly surprised me, given the amount she prays. When I look at all the answers to her prayers, it makes me wonder why I don't pray more. It wasn't long before we knuckled down to some serious praying for the nation. I will let her tell you about our day elsewhere. Brian, Josh, and Simeon joined me for the penultimate day. We headed for Lydd along the sandy beach, but half way through the day we had to cut inland because of the coastal defences. It turned out that the BBC had been in touch with Vincent at base, and asked him to arrange some amateur footage of me actually walking, and also being interviewed. So it was a good thing that I had friends walking with me. I hadn't realized that Brian and Josh were dab hands with the camcorder. Simeon may have been only ten, but he played a mean game of pool, and prayed as much like a warrior as his dad and older brother.

It was hard to concentrate during prayer, because thoughts of home kept clouding my mind. My body was starting to go into early shutdown. Perhaps my brain had sent a premature signal through to my body that this marathon had finished. Whatever the reason, my limbs weren't moving too well. All the slight injuries I had picked up throughout the walk were making themselves felt simultaneously, and their combined verdict was that there would be a lasting physical outcome of the walk. No longer would my knees allow pavement jogging, or the same standard of footballing, nor would my back permit long-term carrying of anything heavy. On the vanity front, it had taken ten and a half months to build up muscle and physique of which I had become quite proud, but maintaining it would be next to impossible. Never again could I hope to achieve the same quality of golden tan, or a sense of being Tarzan 2. My future efforts would be limited to a two-week holiday / mission trip in warmer climates, and the occasional trip to the gym.

My last night saw the fulfilment of what Phil, Amy and I had discussed a year earlier. I would have a gut-buster of a meal at their place to set me up for the last stint. Dream complete, mission fulfilled – hang on – not yet, one day to go! Phil and Amy had also unknowingly prepared to meet a rather different need. Having lost my toothbrush five days earlier, and been too embarrassed to ask a host, or too lazy to nip to a shop, it was with great relief that I snaffled up their spare Rolls Royce of a brush. With a grand welcome awaiting me next day, I preferred to have neither stained teeth, nor stinking garlic breath.

As I flung back the quilt, and leapt athletically for the bathroom at dawn on the final day (toothbrush in hand), I was conscious of a mixture of emotions. Relief and excitement, anticlimax and fulfilment, uncertainty and expectation, sadness and joy jostled together, as I anticipated my homecoming. As I sat on the sofa, waiting for my sister to arrive, I remember very clearly wondering who I had become, what kind of person was I now, what differences would be noticeable to people close to me? It was with more than a tinge of regret that for the last time I went through the familiar routine of packing my rucksack, putting on hiker's socks, followed by my third pair of trusty boots, setting the sat nav, sampling an amazing cooked brekkie, then finding I had forgotten something and having to pack all over again. I had become a minimalist. I recalled some of the initial contents of my rucksack at the outset of the walk. Bivvy bag, solar powered charger, batteries, sleeping bag, superfluous clothing, spare footwear, supply of books had all been discarded as non-essentials, shedding anything up to 10 kilograms.

The last trek from Lydd to Hythe beckoned, and it was time to take the bull by the horns (and I don't mean my sister!). We had planned to cover the first few miles to New Romney at a brisk rate, so that we could also complete the stretch of coastal path down to Dymchurch where we were due to have lunch at a fixed time, then meet a whole group of walkers for the home straight. Walking east from Lydd the land itself is flat, but don't be misled – this was no stroll in the park. The powers that be had somehow ordained that we must cover a deep shingle assault course. At every step our feet became buried in fine stone, which dropped off at the next stride, only for the process to be repeated mile upon mile. It was as tiring as any of the steep climbs around the coast, and I felt especially for my sister, who was beginning to develop painful blisters. Just as it seemed that this would never end, we suddenly hit solid ground, which by then felt harsh and inflexible to our lower extremities.

We talked about our dreams for the future. Sophie was about to venture off on a God mission to Romania for five months, helping AIDS victims. We prayed into it, and asked for God's voice and clarity. I admired her bravery, but didn't tell her! I questioned in my mind whether she was ready for it. (By the time she returned, I knew which of us was right.) After nearly a year of feasting on other people's quality cooking, and knowing that from the next day it would be back to pasta and cheese prepared in my own kitchen, it was a fitting climax to sit down for lunch provided by my good friends Ken and Joyce.

I had every reason for knowing to what heights of cuisine Joyce could rise, and I had even pre-ordered my favourite menu of melon with raspberry coulis, sirloin steak with peppercorn sauce and all the trimmings, followed by home-made banoffee pie.

The problem with such a banquet is the after-lunch desire for rest and repose. But this was the last day, so finding some extra bulldog spirit was not all that hard, since home was barely five miles away. To my utter delight, just after reaching the sea front for the final stint, I was met by a couple of dozen close friends and family. They all wanted to milk the final glory miles, and get themselves on TV – and see me, of course! Our last few miles needed to be speeded up, as it was February, and starting to get dark. The cameramen wanted a daylight shot of me, along with the other walkers, swanning into Hythe. So we obliged, and got our moment of fame right there on the sea front just before the official end. It felt so odd now, having spent ten and a half months outside battling with the elements, to be faced with the thought that the next few weeks would be spent doing nothing more than keeping dry, getting up late and lazing around the home.

But there wasn't much time to dwell on that – right ahead was the finishing post of the Hythe Imperial. Its steps were swarming with yet more family and friends waiting to give me a rip roaring reception. I couldn't believe how many had showed up to welcome me back. A buffet awaited us all, and the room was packed out with over two hundred people. The roller coaster ride wasn't over quite yet, as I could read the expectation on a sea of faces and realized that I would have to gather together ten and a half months' experiences and share them in ten and a half minutes … all the best! A few days earlier, I had sent some photos to Tom Macgregor, who went right ahead and kindly put together some best moments on the video projector, while we all enjoyed our sandwiches. Next up was my contribution, my legs were tired, and my brain was more than usually dead. Somehow I stuttered through sharing my adventures, whilst becoming aware that I was looking at people I hadn't seen for an age, but who would become my best friends again overnight.

The evening was all over very quickly. To the staff of the Hythe Imperial it may have been merely another event. But for me, and my immediate circle, it was a significant end to a monstrous journey, and a fresh beginning to whatever might lie ahead.

CHAPTER 5

The Best Laid Plans Go Where?

Divine appointments

These true stories are by far the most amazing adventures I have had a chance to be part of so far, and as I write them it still feels like they happened yesterday. As you read, you might find some bits hard to believe, because they are not your experiences. They belong to me, first hand. Over the years, I have enjoyed listening to others share their stories about the personal things God has done, but it is not the same unless you own them. Take doubting Thomas, for example. All his mates had seen Jesus re-appear after having been raised from the dead. But Thomas didn't believe, because he didn't see it for himself. When Jesus showed up, it all changed. We need our own answers to our own prayers! So, at the very least, what I'm hoping that this chapter will do is to get you saying: "I'm not sure whether I believe what I have read, but if it's true then I want some for myself!" And, to balance all that up, please remember Jesus' words when He appeared to Thomas: *"Blessed are those who have not seen and yet have believed"* (John 20:29).

Only if his name is Baz

OK, pull up your boot laces and prepare to believe. I'm aware that I may lose some of you in telling this account. It was very early doors, and an uneventful day in the grand scheme of things. But, as I prayed for a word of knowledge, I did think I heard God say the name Baz, and I became convinced that I would meet someone by that name. Majorly disappointed when this did not happen, I eventually finished the day wondering if I had heard wrongly, not trusted enough, or made the whole thing up.

The following afternoon, as I was walking from Herne Bay to Sittingbourne, I came through Whitstable, where I met a man working on the outside of his house. He shouted across to me and asked, "Whereabouts are you walking?" So I told him that I was going right around the coast of Britain. "Righty-o," he replied, somewhat perplexed. "What are you doing that for?" I had two options at this point, both of which were technically true. The cop out was to say I was doing a sponsored walk, or the brave answer was to admit it was a prayer walk. I went brave. "Righty-o," he said again. "Are you one of those?" I thought that he must mean a Christian, so I said "Yes!" To which he responded: "Are you one of those *ones?*" I assumed he was asking if I was a practising Christian, so I nodded. "Hmmm," came the reply, "I've heard that people like you can help people like me. I've got a poltergeist in my house. Can you come and get rid of it?"

Now it is not every day you get that, is it? I wasn't even sure I believed in the things, so how on earth was I going to get rid of this one? I didn't know whether the whole incident was a red herring to distract me from walking, or not. At that moment, for some reason I thought – "I wonder if his name is Baz?"

"That's it," I decided. "If by some miracle his name is Baz, I will try and sort it out. If it isn't, I'm getting the hell out of here!" Guess what? His name was Baz – no way! I was kind of hoping that it wasn't.

We went into his home, and sat down. My head was more than spinning with all that had just happened. Composing myself, I asked Baz how he knew he had a ghost in his home.

He said that things would lift off the table and fly into walls. A weird mist would arrive, lights flash across the ceiling, and a bad smell fill the house. He believed it was something to do with his dead wife haunting the house. OK then, now I was really freaked out. I started praying, eyes open of course, and then it all kicked off. The first thing I noticed was the disgusting smell. I was looking everywhere, still doubting, wanting to know where it had come from, then the lights – flashing all over the ceiling – that was all I needed! I shouted at whatever it was to go in Jesus' name, and it went!

Peace descended on the house, and Baz felt great. He wanted to find out more about this Jesus, and so did Mike, a fella who was working for him and had come round for a cuppa. They were both so open to Jesus, and accepted a couple of *Knowing God* tracts. We prayed together before I left, still somewhat shaken, but overcome with happiness for those two guys.

When the wrong number is right

From time to time, friends from back home would phone for a catch up, to see how I was doing. One morning I got an unexpected phone call from a friend called Steve, who is connected to the church, but who I hadn't seen for quite some time. Funnily enough, he wasn't supposed to be phoning me at all! In fact, he was dialling the number for Sea-View Services, to book a ferry. He didn't even know my mobile phone number. For the sceptics among you, the two numbers are in no way alike.

I picked up the phone, and this guy said; "Hi, is this Sea-View Services? I would like to book a ferry, please." I replied, "Sorry, I can't help you; this is Gary." Then I heard a shout of astonishment. "Gary Lamb?" "Yep, that's me." He then explained who he was, and we had a really good chat about all kinds of God stuff. It was a divine appointment, and God had dialled the number. I later found out that Steve had promptly put the phone down, pressed re-dial and found himself talking to Sea-View Services. He was gob-smacked and felt that he was part of God's plan for that day.

Witness in Maccy D's

I was in a somewhat run-down area near the Cleveland coast. You may be able to suggest numerous possibilities! The previous night my hosts had been reading about helping those who are shunned by society at large. The passage from their book was about a man who used to go out and pray that God would send him the "worst of the worst". As I was listening to the story, I felt that I had been having it all a bit easy. My conversations had been mainly with those who had seemed to be the most approachable, like old ladies at bus stops. I have since found out that that is not always true anyway! Surely it would be a doddle to pray that God would send me a "worst of the worst" sort of person. I became sure that after praying nothing would actually happen anyway, leaving me let off the hook.

Finding myself at Macdonalds for lunch, wolfing down some chicken nuggets, I felt prompted to repeat that prayer. Well, I never! In no time at all, Dave was sitting at my table. "Unusual," I thought, as the restaurant was only half full, and he could have sat at an empty table if he wanted. We got talking, and it didn't take long for me to realize that Dave was the answer to the prayer. He was in a really bad way. Dave has been a heavy heroin addict for the last twelve years, which I'm told is about the rough life expectancy in such cases. Having bought him a milkshake, I listened to him for the next couple of hours.

Dave's life story is a living nightmare. He was making a real effort to stay clean. After lasting three days so far, he was in dire need of a score. I told him about Jesus, and how He can help. Dave's eyes lit up, he needed hope, but also to get out of the area, because people were after him. So I took him to the bus stop, and paid the driver the fare. Dave left, clutching a tract, and saying, "I'm gonna give Jesus a try!"

Although he has my web card, Dave has never made contact since. I fear the worst, but what I do know is that I was destined to meet him, and to share about Jesus before it was too late.

Salvation at the border

I came to treasure my rest days. This time round I was in a Christian retreat near Berwick-upon-Tweed, a gorgeous setting with a breathtaking garden with all sorts of birds coming and nesting there. The one slight flaw was a boxer dog, which I steered well clear of. Let's just say it was bouncy! In the picturesque conservatory, I met two ladies who were staying at the retreat. Manju's Christian neighbour had not been able to make it, so at the last minute she had invited one of her other friends to share a relaxing weekend together. Pamela was not sure about Christianity, and had never experienced God for herself. Although she was a remarkably kind lady, and knew a fair bit about Him, she wasn't overly interested. Until – that is – Manju and I started talking about past reality encounters with God. Pamela's ears pricked up, and she wanted to hear more about this Holy Spirit. I felt moved to pick up a nearby guitar (how embarrassing!) and started strumming gently, asking God to reveal Himself to Pam. In no time at all, she was filled with His presence, and wanted to commit her life fully. She had never believed that God could love someone like her, but that evening He proved it, as she felt the warmth of the Holy Spirit surge through her body.

Whilst I'm sharing about people surrendering their lives to Christ, this is a good opportunity to mention a phone call that came a mere two days later. James, a friend of mine from

Derby who had walked with me in Grimsby, wanted me to
know that one of his friends had just given his heart to Jesus.

Another link in the chain

I have literally lost count of the number of times that God
used me in order to cause two complete strangers to meet. If
you like, I was the middle-man. In Aberdeen I'd arranged to
meet up with Ben, a friend who had ventured out this way
to go to uni, and because he felt God call him to do so.
Unfortunately Ben wasn't able to put me up for the night, so
Vincent looked elsewhere, and found Graham, a man from a
different church, who in turn found me a kind couple to stay
with. However, I did manage to pop down to the pub and
meet Ben. We had a catch-up, and I told him some miracles
I had seen so far whilst walking. He was consumed with
a vision to set up a 24/7 boiler room, which is a room
specifically designed for continuous prayer. The following day
I met Graham, who shared the same passion for prayer, and
instantly knew that the two must meet up. I gave Ben's
number to Graham and they are now friends, working
together to see God make Himself known in Aberdeen,
through prayer. Isn't that so God?

Lunch in Gardenstown

Surely I'm not alone in having the occasional "can't-be-
bothered" morning, where you wish you had not woken up.
My misery was compounded, when I drew back the curtains
to see the rain coming down in sheets. It took every ounce of
will-power to get out of the door. I'm convinced that within
just a few minutes I was more sodden than any proverbial
drowned rat. The inclines around Banff were spectacularly
energy-sapping, and the scenery incredible – great! But
enough was enough, especially when I realized I had

neglected to load up with a packed lunch, or sort my route out for the day. The fact that it was entirely my own fault did not improve my attitude, either.

I trudged along mindlessly, moaning at God the whole time, which makes you feel a whole load worse, because He is completely and utterly perfect. Lunchtime found me hungry, wet and cold, and there was not a pub in sight. I was beat up outside and in, close to tears, and feeling alone, and rejected. I saw a sign saying, "Gardenstown – 1 mile". My GPS insisted that this hamlet had an inn, so I took the extra detour, all one thousand seven hundred and sixty yards of it.

No pub could be seen, so I popped into a little Post Office which was actually open, and made enquiries. "Sorry, dear, there used to be one, but it's not there anymore, and everything else is closed for the day." I dragged myself outside, dejected and soggy. Yes, still alive but only just, or that's how it felt. At this defining moment, I uttered a prayer that I will never forget, because it was so me-orientated! "God, can you find a way of fixing me some lunch?"

I hadn't got to "Amen" in my prayer, or anything spiritual like that, when a car driver pulled up alongside me, outside what turned out to be her own house. A lady wound down her window, and asked if my name was Gary. To say I was surprised would be an understatement. Here I was, in the middle of nowhere, half-way up the east coast of Scotland, hundreds of miles from home, and my name was being called out from a car window!

"Yes, I'm Gary," came my somewhat stuttering reply, whereupon she smilingly invited me in for some lunch! I must admit I made sure that I polished the meal off before troubling to find out how this lady knew who I was. Shirley is a Crusaders' leader who had read an article which included my website details. She had been regularly following the itinerary, and my daily blog. Even though she knew that I wasn't scheduled to pass her way, Shirley had awoken that morning with the prayer that she would get a chance to bump into me, so she could fix me some lunch.

Life saver

In Cullen I got an email to tell me the good news. About two months previously, I had bumped into Joan and her husband whilst walking. They were outside, trimming their hedge. Seeing all my gear weighing me down, they very kindly invited me straight in for a cup of Rosie Lee. I shared with them the reason behind my decision to do the walk, and they seemed genuinely interested, although Joan was very clearly anti anything Christian, and made it clear that she didn't like being Bible-bashed.

We spent a good hour together talking about life, work, and pleasures; it was a great time. Joan insisted on dropping me off a bit further down the road. How could I resist? As I hopped out of the car (only a bit further on, truthfully) I said, "Joan, I know that you don't like people preaching at you, but I feel that I need to say this one thing. 'Joan, God loves you.'"

The Cullen email was all about Joan having had a recent operation, where she was given a fifty-fifty chance of survival. She pulled through, and wanted to thank me for what I had said. As she came round after surgery, they were the key words continuously going round and round in her head, and brought her much needed comfort.

One space left

This ranks up with one of the walk's most embarrassing moments, as well as a God-appointed miracle. During my stroll towards Blackpool, and without noticing it, I must have somehow jarred my back. Unknown to me, the rucksack had somehow masked the pain, as it held the damage all in place. So I walked through the front door of my latest hosts, whom I had never met before, and removed my bag. Wham! I collapsed at their feet clinging onto the stair banister, as my back went into spasm. Imagine how foolish I felt, as I let out a yelp of pain. Bless them, John and Val took it all in their stride as they sought to help.

To my utter amazement, it turned out that Val had an appointment the next day with her osteopath, and she said that if necessary I could have her slot. She attempted phoning, but there was no answer, so she said she would try early the following morning. The night was a painful one, as my back continued to lock up and cause pain. Val phoned in the morning and got through. There was one space left for me, because seconds earlier someone had phoned to cancel their appointment anyway. Also, Val told me that the osteopath was a Christian, which was a nice touch, I thought. I had managed to trap a muscle, which was in turn causing the spasms. So my new-found friend and deliverer manipulated my back, until it crunched like an old creaking door, thus unlocking the pain. I was free, and felt much better for it! I took a rare day off, and was out walking again the following day, albeit without the rucksack!

Are you thirsty?

Nathaniel joined me for a day, as we strolled around the outskirts of North Wales, which can easily be mistaken for Scouser-land. We had a great walk, but it was very hot and stuffy, and for some unknown reason water bottles had been left unfilled. We were beginning to get a bit parched, to say the least, and massively dehydrated. There was not a lot we could do, as our route for the day was mainly going through random fields, and occasionally popping out on to the main road to escape lively cows and their young. Suddenly, in the middle of one of our road-walking sections, a car pulled over and two carers got out of their car, having decided to have their lunch break right there on the roadside. They popped open the boot, and started tucking in to their grub.

Seconds later, Nathaniel and I arrived, having desperately prayed that we would find some water. Completely "off her own back", one lady decided to ask if we would like a drink. Not only that, but she and her friend went on to stock us up with other goodies. It was so good to feel the refreshing water on my crisped-up lips, swiftly followed by downing a chunky Kit-Kat which hardly touched my mouth, backed up with yet more re-energizing fruit juice. We had our fill and got moving, knowing that we had just been looked after by the "Man upstairs", and two unsuspecting carers whom He drafted in.

When someone needs a shoulder to cry on

I'm sure that I'm not the first to say, and certainly will not be the last – Rhyl seafront is not such a nice place, especially during the winter shut-down. Still, I needed somewhere to eat, and that bench seemed as good as any. Then Gail sat down next to me, a bottle of the old bubbly in her hands, clearly more than a bit tipsy. She was a middle-aged lady, quite posh, and well spoken, but wearing her jimjams.

I had become accustomed to seeing drunks, but not like Gail. She enquired what I was doing with that massive rucksack. I told her where I had come from, and where I was going. She didn't believe me, but carried on with some more detective work – "Why are you walking all over the place?" I answered again, but she still remained suspicious. I changed tack, and asked what she was doing in her pyjamas, and why she was drunk at lunch time. She had fallen out with her husband, and the drink was her consolation.

As I told her about Jesus, Gail became very tearful. Some days earlier, and in quite a state, she had been to a church as a last resort, and had asked God for a sign. I was her sign. Gail said that she had to go, but that I must wait for her on the bench until she came back. She said about popping to the supermarket, and I wrongly assumed that it was to buy more alcohol. In fact, it was to buy me a "Thank-you" card. An emotional time followed, as Gail continued to open up about her life. Before long, Craig joined us – another drunk, already homeless at nineteen. Craig was what you would call a more stereotypical "alcy". After the initial hard-man front had melted, more tears flowed, as he began to share the life story of one scared little boy, who had wrapped himself in a protective layer of violence and abuse. He had simply been trying to please his dad, who was now in prison.

Craig sounded brave as he talked about wanting to follow in his dad's footsteps, but the fear written all over his face belied his words. He wasn't cut out for this, and he knew it. Gail and I ended up giving him advice. There was boldness and confidence in my heart, as I told Craig about the new start available in Jesus. We talked about people who could help him. Gail, now sobered up, decided that she needed to get on the bus with him, and find him a place to live and work. I hope it was a happy ending!

When the time is right

I arrived in Bangor ready to meet up with Dan. For a change, this was a host whom I vaguely knew from previous meetings at various Christian conferences. When I got there, I found out it was a student house, and felt immediately at home. I met all the guys, each of whom was really different, yet they got on so well! The housemate nicknamed "Angry Tom" intrigued me. What was he doing, in a house full of Christians? It must have felt weird.

Anyway, Tom was the sort of fella who was the life and soul of any party. He shared my love of football, and we got on well. Dan and I wanted him to come to church with us, but a two-part deal had to be struck. There was a certain young lady on whom Tom was keen, and we needed to ensure that she would be in church at the same time. Then we must watch him play football. Everything sounded good, and the deal was done! Tom walked through the church doors with us on Sunday morning, like Romeo looking for his Juliet. The service began, and still there was no sign of Cinderella coming to the ball.

However, to my surprise, Tom was really moved by the worship, and entered into it. The girl of his dreams strolled through the door part-way through the service, at which Tom's eyes lit up, and all was well. I watched him play footie later on in the afternoon, and quite enjoyed myself, although I was a bit under the weather. I was desperate to get on the pitch, and show the Lamb flair, but sadly didn't get the chance. Later that night, when I should really have been in bed, resting my body for the next day's onslaught, Tom wanted to know more. We chatted into the early hours of the morning. I shared my story of how I became a Christian, which Tom related to. He kept saying that he needed God to reveal Himself. What I was saying was all good, but Tom wanted a sign. We prayed for God to show Himself, and I went to bed knackered!

Five minutes later, Tom got his sign. Shortly before going up the stairs, he found his eyes drawn to a printed tea towel, and saw the word "reveal" stand out, staring at him from amongst the other words. That was it; that was all he needed! Later that day, I found out that Angry Tom had become a Christian. When I left, he gave me this poem.

He wrote me a rap. "S**t" in this rap means good stuff. I didn't want to change his words.

"Lord, I met an amazing man,
taught me s**t about the masterplan;
walking over plains, getting drained through pain
proceeded to walk the lane, learn the game.

I need to see it, a person who changes,
I need to feel it.
So many parts to the puzzle;
fitting them together – causing me trouble.
I wish the traveller the best on his conquest;
maybe He has opened a door for me – a new guest."

CHAPTER 6

Give Us Each Day

Who supplies?

God has been my source from the start to the finish of this epic journey, and I give Him the credit for that. From time to time He miraculously supplied me with food, accommodation, and close friends along the way. Not only has God been my personal supply, but through Him I've become a lifeline to others in need. Sometimes He sent me to the desperate, other times it was just 'coz He likes showing people that He loves and cares about them. In this chapter I would like to share some of those stories and encounters.

Talking of provision, my church raised £5,000 to "give out along the way", and also paid me half a year's wages to cover personal food, equipment, and accommodation support, plus a few ongoing bills. In addition, I benefited from many generous individual gifts. A lasting memory is Ray's kindness in buying me yet another pair of hiking boots, though at the time we hardly knew each other.

God honours good savers

One morning Ross, the son of my Girvan host, came and sat next to me in church. Immediately I had a sense of needing to give him some money, because he was saving up for something special. There followed the usual internal debate one gets at such times. "Lord, first I need to know whether Ross is good at saving."

How could I hope to find that out? True to form, I promptly forgot about the whole thing, and carried on with the meeting. Later that day, we sat down for a scrumptious roast dinner, and ended up talking about money. To this day, I can't remember how on earth we got on to the subject, but the moment of miracle finally arrived. Someone said, "Ross is really good at saving, in fact, he is putting all his money aside for a computer." That was all I needed. God had confirmed it, and I was to give a gift towards this dream.

It's better to give chips than receive them

After saying goodbye to my dad in Wick, and before needing to hop on the bus (only to get me back on track!) I decided to pop into the chip shop. My ever-growing stomach was in need of a top-up. God started communicating to me about how He loves to give good gifts to His children, even more so than earthly fathers. You may know the relevant Bible passage. The chippie noticed that I had a hench rucksack on, and asked where I was going. So I told him about the mad adventure. He decided that the least he could do was to give me some free fish and chips. Grateful for my gift, I headed back towards the bus stop, where I met a lady who started chatting. About halfway through our conversation, I was starving, but I thought that it would be rather nice of me to offer her some of my grub. I was half-expecting her to say, "No, it's OK," but she took the whole lot! To my surprise, I found it really made me feel happy me to give a complete stranger a free present of something I really wanted. Those who know me, and are aware of the rapacious demands of my belly, will appreciate this all the more.

Idy to the rescue!

I'd only been travelling about a week when my first real nightmare scenario occurred, just as I was approaching

Westcliff-on-Sea. My not-so-reliable GPS satellite navigation system decided to crash. Since the route to my host's home was saved on it, and nowhere else, I didn't have a clue where to go! The obvious first step was to phone home to base, but it was one of those rare occasions when absolutely no-one was there to give advice. The previous day Idy, a complete stranger, had been in touch with me via my website, and we had arranged to meet up at the pier to pray around the area. We did this, and enjoyed a fantastic time together. Learning of my predicament, Idy asked who my hosts were due to be, and it turned out that Richard and Ruth just happened to be good friends of his. He knew exactly where they lived, personally walked me there, and also felt moved to give me a very generous gift.

But there was more! Guess what Richard's job was? Computer problem solving! Although he couldn't totally handle this one, he was at least able to diagnose the problem. A phone call to John Rawlings, back in Hythe, brought him up real quick. Yes, thankfully he didn't select the snail's pace at which he swans around the badminton court, so everything was rapidly sorted. Between Richard and my good mate John, the GPS was sorted. On Monday I was back out walking, feeling really valued and looked after by God. He had taken care of every issue for me.

God's sovereignty works through silly mistakes

Some days the route was so simple I felt my GPS wasn't necessary. After all, how hard can it be to keep the sea on your right? Well, one morning I woke up and set off absent-mindedly in the wrong direction. Plonker, I know! For sure, I was tired, if you'll accept that excuse. After about five minutes the error of my ways became more than obvious. So I turned round, which meant I was to be ten minutes later than I would have been at any given point throughout the rest of the day's walk.

Six miles further on, I saw the remains of a devastating car crash. Four police cars were there, a couple of ambulances, and the sirens on the fire engines were still going strong. The realization that I had missed that crash by just ten minutes shocked me – scarily there was no pavement for pedestrians on that road. I could have been a goner, but God protected me and worked through my silly mistake!

It's nice when the sun shines on you

When it comes to praying about the weather, I'm never too sure. You can generally guarantee that – if you are praying for sun – someone not too far away will be praying for rain, and vice versa. Also, my faith doesn't usually stretch that high! To see big things change you still only need a mustard seed of faith, but even that is probably too large for some of my requests, especially where weather is concerned.

On this particular day, my sole wish was that the rain would stop hammering down. This was partly because I knew that I was due to venture over the Humber Bridge, which I had been looking forward to. The nearer I got, the thicker the fog became – but I really wanted to be able to take some photos. I prayed a throw-away prayer, desperate to see the vista of God's creation from such a unique vantage-point.

Well, I had not reached the middle of the bridge before the mist melted, the rain stopped and the sun burst through the clouds. But at the other end the rain tipped down again! Don't underestimate what God wants to do for you.

Safely does it

Trev, who doesn't like Christians at all, walked with me for two miles. According to him we are all walking rule-books, have no fun and judge everyone. He did not mince his words

– "You are a miserable lot!" – and I found myself agreeing with him.

Whoops! Was I supposed to say that? Actually, once you got below the surface, Trev was a really nice guy. I saw it as my mission to help him to understand that God created fun. All I can do is hope that the message made it through. We Christians have a lot to answer for, don't we? Joy is supposed to be our strength.

Now before you think I'm going off on one, trying to preach, there was more to Trev and this story than meets the eye. His reason for volunteering to walk with me was that he knew I was about to venture through a well-known dodgy neighbourhood. He wanted to protect me and my belongings, and he was sure I would have probably been mugged walking alone with all that gear. I'm glad I met Trev, not because he was built like a tank, but because he cared, and that moved me. Also, I was grateful that God had planted him there to guide me, even before I knew that I would need help.

Food glorious food

On the rare day I would go for a deliberate adventure, knowing that I had no packed lunch, and that there were no pubs on the way. At other times, it was just that I clean forgot to plan for food. It was a clean-forget day walking from Newburgh to Peterhead. Towards lunchtime hunger pangs decided to kick in, so I silenced the voice of pride that said, "Don't you dare knock on a stranger's door." and did just that!

The response was far better than I had expected. I met Edward, a devout Christian who had been in the prison service for thirty years. We chatted for over an hour, both feeling comfortable in one another's presence. It was a special time, and we were able to pray together, and put the world to rights. And, as we were doing so, we ate!

When God blesses back

Charlie and Eileen had kindly left me with a substantial gift the night before I was due to set off. As I woke, I started praying that God would bless them for the way they had so generously given towards the walk. No sooner had I trudged downstairs – still half asleep – than I heard a knock at the door. It was friends of theirs, who had arrived with a gift for them. No, it wasn't their birthday, or anything like that, simply a random gift.

Now, I don't go for the "Give something away, then you will get more back" or "Give me a fiver and your arm will be healed" approach. I believe that is utter rubbish. It wasn't in their hearts to seek for a return – their sole intention was to give, and make me feel special. When you behave so unselfishly, you can't help but get God's attention.

Three days in a row

I have lost count of the number of pubs where I stopped off for a quick pint, or some lunch. Well into treble figures, that's for sure! However, occasionally I planned to get a pub lunch, but forgot to draw any money out of the cash point. You see it is not as easy as you may think. Up in Scotland, you can go days without seeing a cash point, and some of the more remote places won't take a card, so it is easy to run low on the loot.

Most of the time, I had a few pounds jingling around in my pocket for a pint. I must big up the Scots here, because three days running I wandered into their pubs pretty much penniless, apart from a bit of drink money, and was treated to lunch without ever mentioning the subject. They saw the rucksack, asked what I was doing, and immediately offered food. Not once did I receive a free lunch in England. Also, while I'm on the subject of bigging up the Scots, many more of them would offer lifts – not that I took them! Then they would chat, without rushing off. Maybe in the future, as a reward for their kindness, God might help them out a bit more in football, rugby, cricket, athletics . . . and the list goes on!

Right on cue

Now and again, the distance between hosts' homes really was too much to walk in one go – and there is not much of a bus service on the far north coast of Scotland. It didn't help that I'd spent a large chunk of that particular afternoon in a café, chatting to the locals about my adventure. I'd begun by talking to just one table of people, but before long everyone had their seats turned towards me, listening to my stories. Where had the time gone? I was certain to be very late in getting to my hosts, but didn't want to trouble them.

So I did what no walker should do – prayed for a lift. Not once did I hitch-hike throughout the walk, but once and once only I did pray for a lift. Seconds later, a car pulled over, and the driver asked where I was going. I told him, and he got me to my hosts right on time! Please forgive me; I had already walked over twenty miles that day!

You stay where I put you

Barely ever did accommodation fall face down, and that is a credit to Vincent and the support team. There was a time, though, when Vincent phoned to say that it had, and together we decided that it was time for a faith adventure. We had been talking about it for quite some time before this.

I set off, and – as you can imagine with a wuss like me – I was worrying about it continuously. The nearer it got to the end of the day's walk, the more anxious I grew. Who cared if it is was a gorgeous day there on the west coast of Scotland? I didn't fancy sleeping out alone under the stars. After covering an average day's distance, I saw a B & B. There were not many about up this way so I assumed it was God's provision, only to discover that it was fully booked. Oh no! What was I going to do? I'd walked a further few miles down the road when suddenly a voice came from the bush!

No, it wasn't on fire, and it wasn't God speaking. The voice said, "I know where you stayed last night." It was a man named George, a cousin of Rhea, with whom I'd stayed a day earlier. He was out doing some gardening. Funny thing was, the front garden was quite small, and the chances of him being out there at the same time as I walked by were more than slim. I stayed for a cuppa, and they kindly offered me a bed for the night. George told me that they were quite often out at that time of day, and would certainly not normally be doing the garden then. How about that?

Lovely, lovely!

On a walk of this magnitude, there are a couple of dead certs. One of those, at some point, is an achy back. That morning I may have loaded the rucksack incorrectly, stepped down a chunky kerb, or wriggled too much in bed the night before. Whatever the case, my back wasn't feeling too pretty. Day-dreaming along the road, I started to imagine how nice a massage would be. It wasn't really that bad, but sometimes you can work yourself up into a bit of a state.

Anyway, I had even found myself praying that I would receive a massage, crazily selfish I know, but I kind of rudely felt that God owed me one. I pictured a gorgeous young blonde ... perhaps I'll stop there! Well, I arrived at my hosts' home; they were about double my age and there was no Cameron Diaz. But, lo and behold, they did have a massage bed! I was taught to use it and commanded to take full advantage ! This was almost a dream come true, and certainly another prayer answered.

Corns please!

There is another thing you cannot escape – problems with feet! I don't just mean the smell, which at times must have had my hosts close to passing out. Blisters were bad, but after time they subsided. The most annoying thing is those little bugging corns. I had acquired one right on my little pinky toe, which was slowly becoming more painful with every step. If you've ever had a corn, you'll know what I mean! It was Sunday, which meant a lovely rest day with Phil and Maggie, who showed me the sights of Cockermouth. We went for a drive, and a little paddle in the lake. Phil noticed that I had a corn on my foot, and offered to sort it out when we got back to his place. He was a retired chiropodist! Now tell me the chances of all that. One – we go for a rare paddle; two – Phil looks at my feet – unusual; three – he just happens to be a foot doctor. Corn was sorted, and pain was relieved. Thank God!

I will do it anyway

More than once, God showed me that He was my supply line, yet all I did was to throw it back in His face. I don't feel proud of this story, but I should share it because it makes God look even bigger. There is no doubt in my mind that there is an arrow missing in the bow of the Church, and that arrow is the miracle of healing. Make no mistake – Jesus spent a lot of time healing people, and He is the same yesterday, today and forever. I had been reading the book of Luke, and really wanted to be involved in seeing a miracle. All day I kept seeing sick people wandering the streets, but I chickened out of offering them prayer. A blind man with a guide dog walked past – I should have prayed for him! Then I made a deal with God, promising that if another blind guy walked past I would pray for him. The time was too short for me to have forgotten my prayer, before it was answered all too literally. I am ashamed to say that I let this second blind person walk straight by too, because I was scared that if I did pray he would remain blind. What amazed me was that God knew all that, and still the second blind fella came my way.

Sort me, sort others

If anyone out there deliberately gave me food poisoning, then now is the time to speak up. It was a beast – the sickness and the squirts stuck around for a good two weeks. At its worst I had to take a trip out to see the doctor, who gave some medication and advice. Jackie and a friend anointed me with oil. If that sounds a little weird, read James 5. I did feel a little bit better after that. It was a great church, which did good things; not only did they do the spiritual things like praying, but they also helped people practically. I went to see a project that helped the needy. It was a furniture shop where everything was donated free, done up to a high standard, and then sold very cheaply to poor families. The staff also got to have really cool conversations with people who couldn't quite understand their generosity.

Everybody needs good neighbours

Carmarthen saw a little thing called a "dead zone" for my GPS system. It started playing up, and I found myself walking in circles, trying to find my hosts' address for the evening stay. After swallowing my male pride, and not wanting a drop more rain to saturate me, I decided to ask for some directions from the next person I saw. Guess what – it was my host's neighbour on her way home! She walked me directly to the door. When gadgets fail, try God!

No way! Was that a healing?

One thing I desired above everything else on this walk was to see amazing healings on a daily basis. That did not happen, which cut me deep and took me a while to get over. I still don't understand all the reasons why, but God knows. But very occasionally a small "perhaps" did turn up. By now you have probably guessed that I can be a doubting Thomas, and a bit of a sceptic.

I was in Lancaster, fresh from a house group meeting with the local church members. We had been encouraging each other by listing all the answers to prayers we had seen down the years so as to stir up faith, when Simon piped up, and asked for prayer for his back. He had suffered a slipped disk, and was not in a good way. As we prayed, Simon felt warmth all over his back. The pain disappeared, and he was able to stand up without any pain. That was a great day for me.

The meal is on us

I would like to follow that healing miracle with a more down-to-earth provision, simply to show that God is interested in the big and the small details. Ian and Nadia from Preston were two of my favourite hosts, and I will tell you why. Off their own backs they decided that they would like to go the extra mile. They had been in touch with Vincent from back home, and asked him to pass on details of my dream meal, starter, main course, and pudding. I went for melon with Parma ham, followed by a fillet of steak in peppercorn sauce with all the trimmings, and then finished off with banoffee pie. It was possibly the best meal of the walk, though it had many rivals!

It wasn't only that, though; it was something about them. They were so caring towards me and my needs that it blew me away. It didn't surprise me to find out that a mere two years ago they had been involved in planting a church, which had now grown to eighty-five. People from all walks of life turn up, the leaders bring a bucket of sand each week for the cigarette butts. Girls with low-cut tops, who haven't yet learnt to be polite, are on the welcoming team. The ethos is simple – "Love the person into the kingdom first, then look at behaviour later." A familiar quote comes to mind – "People don't care about how much you know, until they know about how much you care." God was truly there in that home!

Talking of homes and hosts . . .

CHAPTER 7

The Heavenly Hosts!

I'll stay at yours

In this chapter I hope to honour my hosts as much as I can. Without them the walk could not have happened in the way it did. I know how I'm wired, and am pretty sure that if I had been required to tent it right the way around Britain I would have returned home unsuccessful after about a ten days, soaked to the skin, bitten to pieces, and emotionally scarred forever. So, thank you! Whether or not I would have put a total stranger up in my home I'm not so sure. You did; you took the risk; and that mattered to me more than you will ever know!

We live in a world where people are becoming more and more suspicious of each other as time goes by, and together you bucked that trend, swimming against the tide of opinion that says, "Look after number one, always play it safe, and stop anyone invading your personal space!" You opened up your homes and your lives to a passer-by. You are part of a lost generation of people who care. Man alive, how we could do with more of you in our churches. You not only looked after me, but you gave me something precious but intangible which is rapidly disappearing as the wheel of the world spins unrelentingly faster, and harder.

I'm vaguely reminded of a story that recalls your willingness, commitment, and blind faith. I heard it first in Africa. There was once a lady street-begging, saying that her baby was dying, and in need of an immediate operation. But the mother didn't have the money to save her child. She sat there in tears, as people crossed over on the other side of the road. ignoring her. Does that remind you of a Bible story? A new Christian, unaware as yet of the scandal that goes on in begging, went immediately to his wallet, drew out every last note she needed, and gave it to her. He was startled when he found out that she was back the next day, begging again. He was to find out that she was there every day, and had been for years. She didn't have a dying baby, it was a trick, and she probably had more money than most, because of her persuasive skills. When asked by his mentor if he had been naive and wrong to give away the money, he replied "No!" adding that if the scenario were to happen all over again, he would still give the money away. He didn't want a guilty conscience – what if the woman really did have a dying baby? He believed in a God who would deal with the lady in the way He felt best.

That man had done his duty in being the Good Samaritan, and you did yours! I hope I came somewhere near to what you wanted me to be. Even if I didn't, don't let me put you off from being outrageously kind again, because one day you will strike gold, and your reward will be great in heaven.

"When you stop to think, the idea that I could somehow sort Gary's accommodation for over three hundred nights was off-the-wall. We'd done something like it for short trial walks in the Fens and South-West, when direct personal contact from me proved best, since people were reassured when phoned by 'the pastor'. But what made us think it could be done for nearly a year, long-distance, whatever? By March 2005 things were urgent! So, full of hope, I got going, phoning and emailing churches here in Kent. It was a pity that, very early on – when phoning within fifty miles of home

– I had to squirm through a conversation which ended like this...

'Let me be frank, pastor! Neither I nor my church would be at all interested in helping you find accommodation for your prayer walker in our town. Nothing you could possibly say will change my mind. The subject is closed.'

Thankfully, the next few months were so full of warm, friendly contacts that this memory became more or less submerged, but its shadow loomed over every initial conversation. I had to face facts. Our church might come up with a few contacts here and there, but mostly I would be searching directories and the internet for churches, and intitiating 'cold contact'. It did not take long to realize that I could not get through without God's warm smile. Some mornings I simply lacked bottle to start again. It was a struggle to pick up the phone, and at such times I toyed with thinking it might be good for Gary to spend a few nights sleeping in a cardboard box under the stars.

At times like these you find out new things about yourself – and it turns out I am plain obstinate. Yes, our God can use this not always attractive characteristic for His own ends. I still wonder if it was better to phone potential contacts first, and offer a follow-up letter or email, or do it the other way round? Who knows? On more than one occasion, the fact that the people I dealt with actually ended up hosting Gary says more about their graciousness than my efficiency. Once I found myself actually apologising to my patient Scottish listener, and asking if we could start again, before I caused any more confusion!

In the office, Joyce kept a wonderful tabulated plan on the computer. To look at it you would think I had run a wonderfully efficient plan throughout. Well, you can fool some of the people some of the time...

In the early days I was really grateful that Pioneer People's *Body Book* included several churches up the east coast, who could be comfortably approached. Initially, I assumed we would always have to locate churches with a similar ethos to ours. (I tried others a couple of times early on, but found myself required by bewildered ministers to define what exactly a prayer walk was!) However, as Gary disappeared northwards, it became increasingly difficult to stick to this plan. Quite wrongly, I still instinctively favoured house churches. I was about to have my thinking broadened. Someone told me about "Find A Church", a kind of internet Christian directory. Great – though little does the webmaster know how many email addresses and phone numbers are inaccurate or out of date, or how many hours I used trying to follow up leads which ended precisely nowhere. However, we were to find some of Gary's warmest hosts in localities which seemed least promising, though often I would need to try several possible contacts before striking gold. One guy, who led a tiny independent church, regaled me with theological lectures during our brief connection, giving me to understand that prayer walks were unsound in principle and practice. But that dear man still found Gary bed and board for a night!

It was a bit humbling, sometimes, to find how much people wanted to help. If a church's members were too few or too old to feel comfortable about offering to put up an unknown young male for a night, they were still not happy to leave things there! More than once, feeling that Christian love compelled them to provide some kind of help, they dipped hands in pockets and paid for Gary to stay in a bed and breakfast instead.

Quite typically I would hear something like one of the following: 'Hello, is that Vincent? We've got Gary coming soon. There's a big, comfy double bed in our spare room. Would that be good enough, do you think? Can we contact him on the day, to make sure he is OK? And please could you tell us his dream menu?' Amazing stuff!

But how can I apologise to the various kind folks from north, south, east or west, who may have thought me a bit off-hand when they very kindly phoned with offers or details of accommodation? How could you guess that – for the whole period of accommodation-seeking – I always had the phone diverted to where I was, and never let it just ring, no matter how inconvenient? No way did I want to lose a deal with a potential host. Yet what, for example, can be said to the kind lady from Suffolk, who phoned one Saturday afternoon (my day off)? At the moment you called I was struggling with a bit of interior decorating, and was fighting a couple of strips of newly applied wallpaper as they gradually peeled themselves from the wall through lack of speedy attention. If my mind seemed to be elsewhere – well, it was a bit, but it was not your fault!

As I look back now, I see it was only God Who brought about a successful result from these efforts, because He was behind and ahead of Gary's vision. It was an honour that He allowed me to be a key player in such an event, and it was also a great blessing to serve Gary in following through what he had unswervingly held on to for years – the call of God for him to walk round Britain."

Vincent Oliver

Since returning home I have emailed everyone of my hosts with this question: "What was it like to have Gary Lamb, the prayer walker, staying in your home?" Below are some clues. Obviously – it goes without saying – they are all nice!

"Gary's visit to me was rather special in a number of ways. He was my first guest as a relatively recent widower. Up to that point, I had never been the most domesticated person, hence he found himself at 'The Cricketers' for an evening meal. I was not sure how we would relate to each other, but we got on so very well. Gary's visit had an incredible effect upon the folk at Singlewell Road Evangelical Church, who were so impressed by his sincerity, and the immensity of the project he was undertaking. They still enquire about his progress.

I am so pleased that he is now the Youth Pastor at his home church, and pray that the Lord will richly bless the work. It is so encouraging to hear a young man saying how much he believes in prayer. I trust he will be able to pass on the vision to many young folk."

David Kendrick

"A busy Friday night, with a last minute invitation to come to meet this guy who was prayer-walking round Britain? Not a usual encounter, and this was certainly not normal. My wife and I were introduced to this guy called Gary, his eyes bright and radiant with the reality of the Spirit of Christ. Conversation, questions, ideas all flowed as we shared the wonders of God. This 'stranger' didn't know it, but God was in the process of forming a calling to prayer and prayer-walking in particular in our hearts. He was an encouragement, and inspiration on the way. Through him, I met with another guy who has a vision for 24/7 prayer. It is awesome how God brings His friends in contact with each other!"

Graham Black – Aberdeen *(the pastor of my hosts)*

"Our memory of having you visit was not knowing what/who to expect, as you can't fully tell from an email! Although – having spoken on your mobile earlier in the day – you sounded normal, if there is such a thing!

We phoned to find your estimated time of arrival, but also to see what you would have liked off our extensive menu, as we didn't want you to have lasagne or curry for the third night in a row!

After you had soaked in the bath and soothed your emerging blisters, it was great to hear how the trip had gone so far. The best thing was to share our visions about how church represents itself to the world, and ways we can maybe change that, by loving them just where they are. We also had in common our prayers to see signs, wonders and miracles.

It was such a 'bummer' that you weren't here over a Sunday, as it would have been great to have you to speak in our church, and to stay longer. Our time together was short, but still long enough for you to sow the gift of money into our kids' new flat. It was such a blessing, in fact it 'blew them away' and gave them such security to believe that they were walking in God's plans. We had to go out while you were staying. But it was great that you enjoyed something from our DVD collection.

After giving you your first cooked breakfast of the day, we packed you off with sandwiches, plus information regarding a better route to reach your next destination. But – best of all – we got to pray and prophesy over you.

It was great to have you and so thrilled that you were successful.

Every blessing, Gary."

Susie Harrington
(Pastor, Christian Growth Centre, Maldon)

"In August 2005, we were contacted by our (then) priest – David Jones – to see if we could give overnight hospitality to a young man doing a 'Prayer Walk' round Britain. We were intrigued, and agreed at once, curious to meet someone whose faith was driving him in this way.

To our delight, a fine young man – very polite, and (as he later proved) possessed of a cracking sense of humour – arrived in Maybole to stay with us.

Our rector came over, and after a hearty meal, the four of

us spent a wonderful time sharing faith, and listening to Gary's account of his journey so far.

When Gary left the following morning, both of us felt that we had been enriched by his visit. In many ways, his journey reminds us of two lines from a great, fairly modern song.

'Here I am, Lord; it is I, Lord;
I have heard You calling, in the night.'

Yours in Jesus"

Duncan and Heather

"... Gary arrived by car and ate us out of house and home before taking the bus ... No, sorry; that's the wrong article ...

Gary arrived somewhat convinced that it rains all the time in Wales – it was November after all. There were several real encouragements, other than Gary himself; he came with me to the local youth group in Ystradowen where we joined in the games. Gary had five minutes to talk about his prayer walk and told us of a miraculous lunch in answer to prayer whilst in Scotland – the young people were transfixed, and several older helpers remarked at how encouraging it was to have a decent young man ... well you know how it goes. Later that evening our rector called with a surprise; enough money to buy new boots, as Gary's had just about had it. God was providing! Take care."

Dale

"I seem to remember that the weather was up to its normal wet and dismal for that time of year in the west Highlands of Scotland. You were certainly dressed for it, though in what appeared like an all-in-one rain suit. You were very quick to settle in and were easy to get on with, chatting away quite happily once you had washed and warmed up. I was very impressed with the planning that had gone on even before the trek had started, and yet more impressed that it had taken you quite a long time to really make sure that this was a God-inspired event, not something you simply felt like doing.

I had been certain that it was right to take you into our home, as all Christians should be united in their love for the Lord Jesus. We should be ready to help each other, especially if we are doing something to further the gospel. I had wondered how you hoped to work for Jesus on this walk, but as you told me about the people you had met on the way, and the questions they had asked, it became clear that this was a good way of meeting and chatting to people.

We were busy in the village, getting ready for the Scripture Union holiday club, and you helped to cut out some parrots that would be used in the Treasure Island craftwork.

I hope I don't embarrass you when I say that you have a very pleasant way of just talking about Jesus, something that I find very difficult to do myself."

Jan

"It was a great joy to have Gary and Vincent staying with us those few days and to be a tiny part of Gary's call from God to pray his way around Great Britain. Also, it was exciting to continue to pray for him afterwards, and follow the rest of his prayer route. We felt that it was a wonderful fruition from God that we had this encouraging action happen in this part of Norfolk, which badly needs an outpouring of the Holy Spirit in reviving, convicting, and saving grace and power. In our church here, since Gary's visit, two wonderful things have happened. For some time, three widowed ladies have received much prayer, support and visits from David, our rector. We have also been making them welcome to our Women's Friendly Hour, and they are now at church every Sunday. When Gary visited, we told him about our 'Rock Solid' group for eleven- to fourteen-year-olds, whose numbers had been static at five for quite a while, and we know he prayed for them. This term, new children are coming every week, and numbers are now up to fourteen, for which we praise God. We believe these are among the 'signs' starting to follow in Gary's 'wake' around Britain. But he may not know all until he gets to heaven."

Robin and Christine

"We wondered what to expect when we agreed to put Gary up for a night, as he neared the northernmost stage of his round-Britain prayer walk. We knew he was in his twenties, but little more about him, whilst both of us are in our eighties, enjoying retirement in Dingwall. However, immediately Gary arrived we sensed we should get on well with him – it would be hard not to!

When he left the following morning, and we watched him striding down our hill, we agreed that there went a real Christian who would – in more senses than one – go places. We are confident that Gary's Lord, who is also ours, will increasingly use this very friendly and natural young man as the years go by."

Henry and Margaret

"It was a dark, cold, wet, late afternoon when Gary arrived at our home in Porthcawl. But this dedicated young Christian brought sunshine and warmth into our home, as he shared his walk experiences thus far. We enjoyed a good Indian meal that evening, and we all laughed as Gary chose the hottest curry to fire him up for his onward journey! We were sad to have to say 'goodbye' the following morning. He came as a stranger, but left as a friend, who we hope will call again one day and stay a while. Thank you, Gary, you are a fine example of a follower of Christ, a privilege to have met you. God bless your continued walk Him every day. We look forward to reading your book! Hopefully you will give a good account of your visit to Wales, where there will always be a

welcome with us. However, should you ever decide to take
to the road again four wheels may be a good idea. With our
love, Gary."

Roddy, Sue and Baz

"It was at the National Leaders' Conference in February
2003 that I saw a young man in his twenties get up and
passionately share his ambition to do something that would
make a difference to this country. It is not uncommon to see
a young man dream dreams, and want to make a difference,
but it is unusual to see them turned into action, no matter
what the cost! That young man has become a good friend of
mine, and his friendship to me has been a blessing. He is
truly an inspiration in this day and age where compromise
is imbedded into our society, and I always come away
challenged every time I meet him. I jumped at the chance
of hosting Gary for a night, and the opportunity of a day's
walk with him was too good to miss. When he arrived at my
house he said that he had walked ten miles out of his way to
come and stay with me, but as soon as he sat down and
mum served up her special Sunday roast (especially for
Gary) he said that it was worth every step! We shared a beer,
and I listened to the awesome things God had done on the
first half of the journey. I couldn't help but think that Gary
was fighting a battle with every step, taking ground off the
enemy that he would never gain back.

The next day we walked the twenty miles together, praying
and chatting until the ever reliable Sat Nav guided us up a
grass bank into the centre of the British Steelworks
surrounded by trains and lorries. It wasn't long before we
were being escorted off the premises by security, who I
reckon thought we were two loonies escaped on day
release, as we were dressed in hiking gear, in the middle
of Britain's largest steel works and telling security that Jesus
loved them! It was an amazing day, and I was exhausted

after one day of walking, I don't know how Gary did a full ten and a half months of it.

I look back to 2003 and think it is incredible what can happen when you start by dreaming a dream!"

John Broughton

"We met Gary at Ron and Wendy's house, along with our two noisy kids, and found it a very enriching evening hearing him speak with great conviction about his faith and about the walk. It's always good to have fellowship with each other and hear other people's stories. We particularly remember your prayer before meals, to the tune of 'The Adams' Family'. Our kids still sing it with great gusto, very often, and talk about how you taught it to them! Completing the walk is a real achievement, one that you will draw on for the rest of your life, and also for your new job."

Pippa and Chris LLoyd (with Toby and Rowan)

"As Gary's time staying with us in Lowestoft went by I felt inspired both by him, and his motivation to the huge task of walking around our wonderful land. My husband, and son James were equally found of him, especially when we all went to watch James' cup final in the under 16's Norfolk and Suffolk football youth league. Gary was pleased because the game went to penalties, and James was a happy chap too, as he took home his winner's trophy, and man-of-the-match award. James talked to Gary about having to choose between two football teams, and we all realized that Gary not only has great listening skills, but also connects well with people of all ages. When Gary left us for his onward journey, I realize that he had shown huge interest in us as a family, and also in our pursuits – but I hadn't taken the time to find out anything about him, apart from the walk. Since then, this is something I am always conscious of when talking to others. We are sure this experience and adventure will remain with Gary forever, and we are glad we could help him along the way."

Lis, Malcolm and James Bryant

" 'We seek him here, we seek him there...' As I drove along the leafy lanes of east Essex, the *Scarlet Pimpernel* rhyme flashed across my mind. Surely Gary could not have got lost?
He hadn't!

I returned home to find one round-Britain walker, drinking tea and chatting away with my family as if they had known each other for ages.

'Did you get lost?' inquired my other half.

Cheeky blighter!

Apparently Gary had taken the direct road to Harwich, and there was me thinking that he would opt for the picturesque route. Our immediate topic of conversation was Gary's sore foot, which had been carefully tended the previous night when he stayed with Catherine in Colchester. Clearly Gary needed a rest, so he took a bath and some food, which seemed to rejuvenate him, and we all enjoyed yarning with each other. Next day, 14th April 2005, dawned cloudy and cool. Since the local river ferry was not yet functioning, I took Gary road to Felixstowe by road where we met up with Norman from Gary's home church. I so enjoyed their company that I stayed with them as long as possible, talking about church, and Crusaders, and prayer buses, about scenery and feet, and awful jokes. Can't wait to read the 'Gary Lamb Chronicles'."

Nigel

"Meeting a young man like Gary gave us such joy and hope for the future. It's a shame that people only hear about the bad things that some young people get up to, rather than the good that is done by others. They end up all getting tarred with the same brush. We knew roughly what time Gary would arrive in Tenby, so we aimed to be home in time to meet with him. It was a right miserable day, howling wind, pouring rain and very dark. As we pulled up, there – twenty yards in front of us – was this wet bedraggled person with a rucksack on his back. Somehow, we guessed that it must be Gary.

However, although our house number is 15 we were not in time to stop Gary from mistakenly knocking on number 16! When we finally reached him, he was on the doorstep of the young girl next door, trying to explain to her that he was supposed to be stopping there for the night! The young lady's face was a picture, but it was alright after a bit of complicated explanation.

So that was our introduction to Gary – a heap of sopping wet clothes walking through our front door. He did improve a bit in appearance, after a hot bath and one of Louise's roast dinners. The trouble was – the evening was not long enough! Time seemed to fly by as we talked about all sorts of things, but it is not surprising that by 10 p.m. he needed his bed. Even though it was for a single night that we met Gary, we felt as if we had known him all our lives. We believe it is the Holy Spirit in Gary that makes people feel that way about him."

Joe and Louise

"We enjoyed planning for Gary's visit, giving him some home comforts and privacy. Prasanna got a chance to speak with him about how we can check whether what seems to be a leading is coming from God, or not. Gary touched on this theme again, when he kindly agreed to be interviewed in our church. Prasanna is researching new ways of approaching the treatment of mental illness, and was encouraged by listening to some insights which Gary was able to share through his own dealings with people back home. Overall, we were delighted to let Gary have the use of our holiday flat, so he could have some time with himself. We would love to see Gary again, if he feels like visiting Whitby – maybe the lure of the spa bath will work its magic."

Prosanna, Sheenagh, Ryan and Lewis

"The people of the Isle of Skye were blessed by Gary's visit, and still pray for him. I believe his coming also produced a definite result. I shared with him a feud between one of my relatives and another man, who on one occasion actually knocked him down and jumped repeatedly on his face. My relative struggled after that, and though the other man was given a short jail sentence he was released not long before Gary came and began a lot of verbal abuse, creating an atmosphere of fear and tension. Gary and I prayer-walked the actual area, and the threats ceased. But something still more unexpected happened in the New Year, when the other man turned up at my relative's door to shake hands and put the past behind them. My relative wasn't in at the time, and when he heard of this visit next morning he was extremely angry, and immediately went round for a confrontation. But, as his wife watched, she saw them shake hands and go into the house together. Two hours later (after a lot of prayer) we were starting to worry, but then my relative came home calm and happy. Everything was fine, and still is."

Ian and Agnes

"Although I was brought up as a Christian, I had no desire to get involved with church. When I left school, all I wanted was to get out into the world. By the time I reached my late teens I was drinking heavily, and twenty years later was a confirmed alcoholic. At this moment of crisis, I cried out to God in my misery. He guided me to Alcoholics Anonymous, where – to my amazement – I found that God could and did lift the desire to drink off me. I had heard of God in the past, but now I had really experienced Him. I had probably always believed there was a powerful Person up there somewhere, but no way had I realized that there is a God who takes a personal interest even in people like me, who have totally messed up. Although I was grateful to God at this point, I still slid back into the world for a couple of years. But the experience left me with a clear sense of un-fulfilment, and eventually I realized that I needed a Saviour. When Gary came knowing that he was due to stay with the minister at Kyle of Lochalsh, he probably didn't dream what background I had. My wife Sheila also had the desire to drink lifted from her in response to prayer, although she did not realize at the time to whom she was praying. But, within six months of this encounter, Sheila not only got back to working as a doctor, and regaining her children's love but also found me – all in six months! Nowadays, Sheila describes prayer as a lifeline. We both had a great time when Gary stayed with us!"

John and Sheila

"I remember Gray coming to a meeting I was at in Lostwithiel, and I told him about how I was healed from ME. I had it for a long time, and the doctor couldn't really help. My friend Tim was really worried about me. We prayed for ages for me to be healed. One night, we were praying as usual at bed time, when I suddenly felt I really had been healed. In the morning all the symptoms of ME had disappeared. This gives me faith to go on praying for my Dad and my sister, who both still have ME. My doctor didn't say anything, but I think he knew that it was God at work. So did Tim, and Tim's mother. I don't think we should ever give up; we should always expect the unexpected."

Chris from Lostwithiel

"It was good having Gary to stay with Reena and myself at our home in Castle Douglas. Gary and I got on very well despite having different beliefs. Although, as a youngster in Wales, I had formerly prayed and attended Sunday school, so far as I was concerned that was something to be simply left behind once I moved out from home. When Gary asked me about my views on evolution, I think I disappointed him by denying that there was a God who influenced the process. When he suggested that the human emotion of love does not fit in with Darwinism, I had to confess that both love and hate were, in my opinion, simply the results of chemical reactions, and the way the brain works within the human body. Gary's purpose in life is to follow his God, whereas mine is to chase the goal of contentment, accepting the theory of survival of the fittest and that we exist solely to perpetuate the human species. Gary seems to believe that there is a God-shaped hole in every human heart, but I don't see it. He tried the old chestnut about there not being many atheists on a sinking ship. Whilst that may well be true, in my view it is just because people want to believe in a higher Power. I would describe myself as an agnostic rather than an atheist, and I was very happy with what Gary was doing, since I think everyone should follow their own convictions. How would you like it to end?"

Brian from Castle Douglas

"Gary brought real life and encouragement to everyone in my daughter's family home, and it was especially good to be able to talk to a prayer-walker about praying. For me, talking to God is something I do every day, and every circumstance. Gary asked me if I could remember any particularly outstanding answer from God. So I told him about a lady we were praying for in an Assemblies of God meeting. She was very ill in hospital, but there was no way she could have her operation, because she kept coming out in a rash, so the nurses just spent their time trying to get her well enough. One day we were all standing around her bed, praying, when a bee flew through the open window, and stung my friend on her head. It appeared to be the exact opposite to an answer to prayer, but God knows what He is doing. The venom counteracted the poison in my friend's body and her rash healed, making it possible for the operation to take place after all. She lived for several more years, and all because of a bee sting. Gary liked that story so much that he got me to tell it again on video."

Eileen from Peterhead

"It was a case of a laugh a minute when Gary was staying with me, especially when I watched him attempting to split logs with an axe. He absolutely could not do it! We did try reaching out to some JWs, but we had to call it quits as we came to a stalemate. So as far as I'm concerned, the purpose of life is to get to know Jesus Christ, since that is the only way to get to heaven. Gary did ask what gets me down in life, but apart from wanting to have a wife (same as him?) there is very little that gets me down. My mum was a great Christian and even though I got into so many holes, and was always in trouble with the police, she never quit praying for me, and finally got me sorted. Prayer has worked for me so many times that I have forgotten many of them. Before I was baptised I had such bad pains in my arms, and the medical authorities actually said that there was no hope of a cure. Funny enough, when I came up out of the water after being baptised, all the pain had gone. Don't tell me that is a coincidence!"

Graham *(from Nairn)*

CHAPTER 8

Having the Last Laugh

God has fun

Children are great at asking questions "out of the blue". I love
the story of the little girl who one morning, over breakfast,
suddenly wanted to know if God really was everywhere. Her
mother attempted the standard quick-fix reply – "Yes, my
darling, of course He is." Immediately, the little girl grabbed
an open jam-jar from the table, slammed the lid on and
exclaimed triumphantly, "Mum! I have caught Him!"

Funny, that – because in the Bible 2 Chronicles 2:6 reminds
us that even the heaven of heavens is too small to contain
God! Maybe, like the little girl, we can only trap the bit of
Him that we understand into our jam-jar. It is the one way to
feel in control. But, unfortunately, we find ourselves unable
to escape, because we are imprisoned beneath the ceiling of
our limited grasp of how big God really is. We catch
occasional glimpses of something greater, and long for a day
when our understanding of God will be uncontainable.
Meantime, may we at least find ourselves using increasingly
bigger jars!

As a new Christian, the idea of a God who has a sense of
humour was way outside my toast-topper-sized jar. Still,
looking back, it feels as if He had actually always been dropping
hints that He, too, likes a good laugh. After all, as my mate
Joe told me, it was God Who invented sea cucumbers, star-
nosed moles and Caribbean mountain chickens! He cannot be

categorized. In fact, just when we think we have successfully
done so, we realize that all we have achieved is to confine Him
into a caricature of what our finite minds believe He is like.

I remember reading *The Screwtape Letters*, by C.S. Lewis,
and understanding a bit more about the tactics of the enemy.
Not only does he try to insert bad thoughts, but he also spends
a lot of time trying to keep the good things out of our minds.
One notion he had stolen from me, until then, was that God is
happy and fulfilled in who He is. I'm confident that God
chuckles a lot, and believe in the deepest part of my heart that
it was He who created humour. Surely laughter, along with
the ability to have loads of fun, originates in Him and comes
from His nature? It seems that the enemy is currently focusing
on getting us to wrongly give him the credit for all the fun and
laughter in the world. As a result, guilt can accompany us
down Laughter Lane, whereas God gave us the gift of joy.

Yes, some things surely stir Him to act against the forces of
darkness, and in such times He does ride out like a mighty
warrior, face set like flint, eyes blazing like fire. It's hard to
imagine a smile on the divine face at such times. When the
King of the hosts of heaven makes a move, He does so for His
glory, and also for His people, such is His desire to see them
come into all that He has destined for them in eternity. When
He's mean, He's often mean for us.

But the God we serve is in charge of the whole world and
takes care of people individually, showing who He is by doing
so simultaneously and magnificently. Our invincible One
knows no defeat! He holds the whole world in His hands,
but still counts the number of hairs on our heads, and knows
what makes us either happy or sad. He communicates with us
one to one, diverse though we are, and is still able to get
through. It makes me so mad when God is portrayed as a
grumpy old-timer, incapable of raising a smile, and sitting idly
on His throne, amusing Himself by burning our butts with a
ray of heat as the sun shines through His big magnifying glass.

This chapter is all about the way I believe God continually communicated with me through my own silly mistakes. It meant a lot to me each day to think that while He watched me He was chuckling and smiling encouragement, as I tried to discover His personal direction. He opts to speak to His children by all sorts of means; in my case, He frequently chose the way of laughter.

I've been through enough bizarre and totally funny incidents to fill a book. I'm a bit sad at having to be selective, but if all my stories were included in this book, it might well become as thick as, and certainly more expensive than the Bible itself. And – unlike God's Word – it would not be 100% inspired by the Holy Spirit!

Uncomfortably low near Lowestoft

At many points around the British coast, out-flowing water – usually a river – meets the sea at sufficient depth to make it impossible to literally hug the coast, unless of course one can walk on water! I guess here and there that ability would have been a big help. Anyway, if you choose your timing correctly, it's easy enough to cross some of those points, since low tide leaves them entirely dry. Needless to say – as I crossed the almost deserted sandy beach close to Lowestoft – I was completely ignorant of any such tidal variations. A man walking from the opposite direction warned me that – a short way ahead – there lay a place about ten metres wide, where the tide was coming in quite fast and meeting an outflow from further inland. His reassuring "famous last words" were ... "It will be fine, though your feet might get a little wet. The water's no more than ankle deep."

On reaching the place in question, I chose to take the precaution of putting my GPS into my waterproof pocket, but with no conviction that it was really necessary to do so. The first slightly nervous step seemed to confirm that all was well

– phew! That guy had said it was shallow, and he was right. But my opinion changed with the second step, on which – wait for it – I completely disappeared, right under! In actual fact, it cannot have been more than chest height, but it took me by surprise. I stumbled forward, and went right in. What a donkey! After just about managing to wade my way across to the other side, my face was bright red with embarrassment, even though the water was freezing. It was the sort of moment you don't want to see anyone else on the beach. However – lo and behold – what should be the first thing to meet my eyes but a rather attractive young lady, walking her dog, and apparently the only other person on the beach! She was clearly in absolute stitches. Thank goodness, it was a sunny day, so I sat down to slowly dry off, feeling sorry for myself, and extremely mad at the man who had pranked me. My pride was battered. The stunningly beautiful young lady finally walked off, still bent over laughing, leaving me alone on the beach, feeling inwardly bruised.

But suddenly, reflecting on it all, laughter welled up inside me, fuelled by the dream of seeing someone else do the same thing. Perhaps it had been a bit dangerous, but it wasn't so bad! I was OK, and would be out walking again tomorrow. In a way, so what! Sitting on the beach, chewing the seaweed about the recent episode, a feeling of joy entered my being. A voice seemed to say, "She needed that!" We all need to laugh sometimes. I was glad to have been able to help make that girl smile, and in fact the whole incident still makes me crease up. I'd overreacted in my heart, but God had allowed me to look at myself, and laugh at the sight! He had begun to teach me a lesson. Don't take yourself too seriously! Relax!

Walking through prison

A man named Dave, who had befriended me at the local church on a Sunday, joined me for the day. As you can appreciate, I tried to be a little more professional when strangers joined me for a stint. So I woke up slightly earlier, and planned the route. Dave is an exceptional man, who has achieved so much, despite losing sight in one eye. He has run nine marathons, competing to a high standard, and earned a black belt in karate (5 dan). He is a freakishly good magician, and has lived life to the max. Dave has suffered abuse, and had a nervous breakdown, but has come through it all. If I'm honest, I felt a bit unworthy being in his presence. At the same time though, he was incredibly humble and gentle. What a man! So the last thing I wanted to happen was for the route to go pear-shaped, and for me to look silly. We were following the GPS route, when somehow we ended up walking through an open prison. The ordnance survey map clearly marked the route straight through the heart of the grounds, so we walked it. On trying to exit the premises, we got stopped by security, and asked what on earth we were trying to do. Surely they didn't think we were prisoners trying to escape, did they?

I showed the guard my map, he nodded and radioed through. We were watched, and ushered unsmilingly from the site. We prayed our socks off as we went through, believing that God had sent us to pray for that place. It didn't end there! The same footpath continued to take us past sheep (who pegged it), cows (who wouldn't budge) and horses (who followed us for quite some time), through back gardens, and eventually to a big, mean beast of a dog.

I was bricking 'em virtually all day. Did even black-belt Dave want to face that brute? Fortunately, we did manage to find another route, avoiding the Doberman's slavering jaws, and finally made it to our destination. I'd learned another valuable lesson: sometimes I need to look and feel like a poltroon; it tends to help me rely on God more. The day ended with me praying far more effectively than when it started!

No way, the joke prayer works

Do you ever find yourself praying, and then not really believing it, but at the same time sort of believing it – just a teeny weeny little bit? Call it what you will – half-hearted prayer, a lack of faith, a dishonour to God, a total and utter disgrace – but it happens, and can get the most surprising, pleasing results. Maybe, in actual fact, it is this kind of prayer that works – prayed in honesty and with a mustard seed worth of faith.

So, the evening this joke prayer took place was at the meal table as I sat with Malcolm, Lyn and James munching some very tasty food. It was my first time with a non-Christian family as hosts, and I was trying to make a good impression. We got on to talking about God and what on earth was the point of prayer-walking right around Britain? I explained the idea, and guessed they probably thought ... "This guy's a bit of an oddball!" ... though they never really made it clear. It was a relief to find that we had some stuff in common, mainly football! So I changed tack, and we started exchanging views about football teams. James had a very important cup final the next day, and asked me to come and watch. The night before, Malcolm had kindly offered to find me a church to go to, but they would not be going because they wanted to watch their son play football. What would be right in this situation – James, or church? James, of course!

Then came my joke prayer. Can you believe it? At that meal table I found myself saying, "Right; I'm going to pray that it will be an exciting game – with goals – that ends in a draw followed by extra time, then penalties, and that James gets man of the match." Where on earth did that come from? Why pray that? I did sort of mean it, but what did God think of that kind of prayer? What did my hosts think about that outburst? Surprise was written all over their faces. Had this guy just prayed at their meal table, right in the middle of a normal conversation?

Next morning, one of Malcolm's special cooked breakfasts awaited me, and any slight awkwardness seemed to have been forgotten. We all climbed into his Lexus, and headed for the stadium. A good number of spectators had turned out to cheer on the teams. To my absolute amazement, the match unfolded exactly as my prayer had said, and ended as a high scoring draw. An exciting period of extra time followed, and then – yes – penalties decided the result in favour of James' team. Now it was time to declare who had been made man of the match. You guessed it – James' name was announced over the PA system. Later on down the pub, it was time to remind James of my prayer, and he was utterly gob-smacked.

Buddha in the bunkhouse

From time to time, I get these particularly "heightened" days spiritually. Does anyone else have experiences when the mere sight of a swaying tree can remind them of the work of the Holy Spirit, or at the other extreme a black cat might mean the presence of a witch nearby? Occasionally, more or less everything can appear to have a spiritual context. It was on one of those days that God showed me something through reality. As you've guessed by now, I did not always have the luxury of staying in five-star hotels. Every now and again I had to "lower myself" to a cheap but not necessarily cheerful bunkhouse – though most of them were fine! On arriving at this particular one in northern Scotland, I had the option out of about a dozen manky beds, and to boldly go where no-one dared any more. Signs of past human habitation were all too evident to my despairing gaze. I seemed to be in a sea of yellow, crusty sheets where more than one person had clearly failed to make it to the bathroom in time. The rusty lockers appeared to have neither locks nor keys. Water oozed in an unattractive dribble from a single shower intended to be shared by up to twelve guys. Having selected the best of a decidedly poor choice of beds, the Indiana Jones inside drove me to daringly risk opening the kitchen door. And, on this day of spiritual alertness, what should hit me between the eyes but an old, faded book? Yes, there on a large, square teak table – apparently the only clean furniture in the whole place – lay the opportunity to learn everything I might want to know about Buddha. In the context of my day, the mere sight of such a book scared me.

I decided to go for a shower after all, although with some fear, given the value of my possessions and the absence of security. But no sooner had I shut the bathroom door than my hair stood on end, as I heard another door swing shut. So I decided to check for who else was around – no-one. This happened three times, before I finally caught sight of a door beyond the dormitory area, also mysteriously opening and closing. But still nobody there! Freaky, or what? On the fourth occasion, I just stood on the other side of the door, and checked the purely scientific explanation which was dawning on me. Yes, I was just creating a through-draught, and it wasn't Buddha or anyone else at work, after all!

And the reality lesson? Simply, don't go through a day looking too hard for meaning in everything; on the other hand, don't go through a day refusing to notice God in the smaller things of life.

When should a monk watch football?

You recall that at Holy Island I was rescued from the grave probability of missing out on the FA Cup Final, through the amazing initiative of two sympathetic brothers with surprising access to a TV. But, for a Liverpool fanatic like myself, a mere final between Man U and Arsenal couldn't be classified as the crème de la crème. Those who recall the match will agree that it was a bore draw to end all bore draws. Nevertheless, a genuinely unbearable sacrifice lay in wait for me, just a few days later. I couldn't imagine how to exist knowing Liverpool were down to play AC Milan for the European Champions' League final, yet no way would I be able to watch. A quick check on my schedule confirmed my worst fears. Two nights of the entire walk were likely to be spent in monasteries. On the evening concerned I was due to arrive at Nunraw Abbey, the second of them!

I know I shouldn't have, but I couldn't help focusing and praying all day for a chance to watch this cup final. The problem was that Nunraw Abbey is in the middle of nowhere, so finding a nearby pub instead didn't seem a realistic option. On arrival at the Abbey guest house, I was solemnly shown to my space. Basic is not the word, it was a box of a room, with a small Bible on a table next to the bed, and that was it. I should, of course, have been ecstatic at the prospect of a night shut up with a Bible and some fabulous grounds to look out onto, but for once (?) my earthly desires were outweighing my spiritual ones. It did help, of course, to know that God Himself supports the mighty Reds, and would be keeping a keen eye on proceedings, Hmmm! I politely asked the monk if there was a chance that there would be a TV anywhere in this massive place. The carefully polite reply came, as from one pilgrim to another, "I'm sorry, sir: this is a monastery." Then the need to ask another rude question erupted in me – "Any chance of getting hold of one?"

My host was blatantly embarrassed, and incredibly surprised at being asked again! Who knows what he really thought of me? But, in typically humble Cistercian fashion, he replied, "I'll see what I can do." Later that evening, at a nail-biting quarter-to-eight and after much travailing in prayer, there came a knock at the door, and a top-secret invite to go and watch the match in a mystery nearby location. At three-nil down, into the second half, I was regretting having bothered. But the Reds' class finally showed. I retired to bed singing tunelessly, but joyfully "You'll

Never Walk Alone", and with the image of Stevie G clasping the Champions' League trophy forever imprinted on my memory. It felt so good that God would respond even to a prayer to enjoy one of life's more earthly passions. Fathers sometimes spoil their children, and so does God. According to what Jesus says in the book of Matthew, the whole point is to ask, and let Him decide.

Why do leaves go brown?

Before starting the walk, I shared about the vision in a lot of schools, and always asked at the end of the presentation whether the children had any questions. There was one recurring theme which more often than not turned my gaze towards the teachers, as they squirmed in disbelieving horror. Yes, you have probably already guessed it. "Gary, what will you do when you need to go, but you are miles away from the nearest loo?" For some reason they never seemed quite satisfied with my simple answer, "I'll just find the nearest woods!"

The realists among you will not be surprised to hear that my first test of bowel containment came pretty early on, whilst still in Essex. It was to give a whole new meaning to David's words, "I'll become yet more undignified than this." Inescapably, there arose a situation where I could no longer argue with my inner workings, which were audibly seeking urgent and explosive self-expression. Fortunately, I was walking through a dense wood at the time, and frankly it wasn't loss of modesty that concerned me – it was keeping skids away from pants. I always knew that God must have had a reason for making mallow leaves so big, smooth, and supple. Nature's answer to Andrex!

If there is a moral to this particular story, it has to be the need to take more notice of the biblical command to be ready in and out of season. Although, as everybody knows, there

are no mallow leaves in winter! So the timing was better than
the readiness.

The Carragher look alike

There are so many people in the world to whom I bear no
resemblance, and high on that list is Jamie Carragher, the
Liverpool centre back. My friends know I look much more
like, say urm Brad Pitt, don''t you?! There is someone in
Britain who to this day really believes that I'm Jamie. It all
started whilst relaxing in Sainsbury's, munching my lunch. A
happy group of Down's Syndrome people came in, accompanied by a couple of helpers. One of them kept smiling at me,
and giving me the thumbs up. I was happy to play his games,
pulling a few funny faces by way of response. Before too long
he got up, and swaggered over to my table, saying loudly,
"I know who you are!"

I thought the fame of my walk had gone before me. Not so!
Who could this guy actually think I was? Then he amazed me
by asking for my autograph. Not wanting to disillusion him
from whatever he was thinking, I took the pen from him, and
simply signed my own name. Without even looking at my
signature, he thrust the paper in his trouser pocket, throwing a
glance of triumph at all his mates as he did so. It was his
parting shot that clued me in to what was going on. "Thanks,
Carragher. Good luck for the game at the weekend!"

What would you have done? The choice was between
blowing his dreams by insisting on the truth, or playing along
with his misunderstanding. All I could think was that I wanted
him to be happy, to go on enjoying the conviction that he
really had met someone famous. So I decided to leave well
alone. He went back and boasted to his mates, whilst refusing
to let them get anywhere near the hallowed autograph. He
continued to smile across, clenching his fists with joy. At
last, to my infinite relief, the party got up and started to file

out with one of the helpers. But – be sure your sin will find you out!

To my horror, the second helper remained behind, and now approached me. Confessing herself to be totally ignorant about football, she nevertheless expressed delight in having found a real live Liverpool player, since both her sons were ardent fans, and would be over the moon if they too could have my autograph! The whole thing had backfired, and my own embarrassment at having to confess who I was paled into insignificance with hers, as she realized she had swallowed his entire story unquestioningly! Maybe staying quiet, when you know you should really speak out the whole truth, can be as damaging as a so-called white lie. It has been well said that the road to hell is paved with good intentions!

Washroom nightmares

Maybe communism does have its good points? Endless rows of indistinguishable apartments, each with the same un-unique layout and facilities, do at least make life easier for the passing overnight guest to find his way about. In ten and a half months I failed to find two identical bathrooms. Let's concentrate on bathwater options to begin with, shall we? One: start with the hot tap till about half full – if the hot lasts long enough – and assume you will be able to eventually cool it down before flooding the entire bathroom! Two: Start with cold tap and rely on heating it later with a dose of near boiling water – could end in a lukewarm bath. Three: Run both taps simultaneously and hope for the best – not great if both taps run at different speeds. Or the rare fourth – alternate a dash of cold, followed by a pinch of hot throughout. On those occasions when I selected option four, it took so long that I'm convinced my hosts were baffled by my apparent obsession with cleanliness! I employed every option successfully from time to time, but more often than not I encountered a mini disaster because each contains a serious element of risk. God bless combination boilers (*not!*). Have you ever prayed for patience, then wondered how God would answer your prayer? Isn't it usually only later on that we see His hand at work in the nitty gritty of our lives? Wouldn't it be great if hindsight sometimes happened sooner, or that we could simply see into the future to see how hot we should run the bath water? Wouldn't that be so much easier? Hang on! What was I saying about needing to learn patience?

Self-invited guest

Well, how was I supposed to know? All I had done was to turn up at this glorified pub-wannabe-hotel, confident that the church office had come up with the goods once again. The first thing I saw as I ambled past was a rather swanky TV lounge on which I set my sights. After the barman showed me to my somewhat modest bed-sit, I partook of a belly-busting meal and dreamed of putting my feet up in that luxurious room whilst watching a good footy match. As soon as I had squared up, I took my swollen stomach with me and settled myself in. Everything imaginable was there for my comfort, and I even took the trouble to hunt around for matches in order to enjoy the extravagance of the available log fire. I made myself a cup of coffee and tucked in to some nearby goodies which had apparently been left for the benefit of lounge users. Having switched on the box, it was a bit disappointing to see Celtic get thumped yet again in a European match, but at least it seemed I had the place to myself. Quite a treat to be alone for once!

So it was with some annoyance that I saw the door swing open and a whole family bundle in. A look of blank astonishment was written across each face. The children crouched to one side, as their parents unleashed fusillades of angry foreign vocabulary to which I shrugged incomprehension. Then – as suddenly as they had arrived – the whole group vanished, only to return dragging with them a totally bewildered barman. It turned out that my presence in that front room was particularly puzzling to him, since it was actually part of the family's personal apartment! I left very apologetically, and scarlet with embarrassment, although at least I had obviously brightened a dull day for the barman. He was plainly struggling to conceal his laughter. It was in some haste that we both made our exit, creasing up, though I still owe that family some matches and biscuits! To this day I'm not sure what the lesson was, but these things happen to me. Please send in your suggestions – no more than twenty words, please! Maybe the solution is for every school to teach Icelandic.

Canute, or Moses?

There was once some guy called King Canute whose courtiers used to over flatter him about his power to command anything. One day, slightly fed up with it, he had them place his throne on the beach, and spent the next several hours ordering the tide not to come in. When the inevitable happened, he simply reminded his followers that some things are beyond the power of the average Joe.

Take another average Joe – Moses. He simply could not string two words together, but with over one million people lined up behind him, stranded on the shore of the Red Sea, pursued by an army of angry Egyptians, Moses just used a wooden stick to command the waters to divide and make a safe way of escape. The key difference was that Moses was cooperating with what God wanted, while Canute was simply throwing hatchets at the moon, as it were.

And a final average Joe – Gary Lamb. You will find it hard to believe how many times I actually commanded the rain to stop right there and then, fully believing. I'm convinced that the Almighty had the odd laugh from time to time, by causing it to rain yet harder, even when I thought it impossible. On those occasions I found myself simultaneously defiant, mocking the worst it seemed He could send, and paradoxically ready to wimpishly surrender, and pack the whole walk in.

Having said that, I do believe there were times when I was perhaps closer to what God wanted to do, and my meteorological commands may even have provoked a positive response. As I look back, I wonder if the point behind all this is the need to pray anyway. At the very least it was a way for God to get me talking to Him – which can't be bad.

Tell it how it is!

Tiredness can overtake us at the most inconvenient moments, particularly when arriving at the home of an unknown host. On the occasion to which I refer, the day's walk had been unusually long and hot, and the symptoms of fatigue must have been glaringly obvious to most. My new acquaintance, a balding man in his late fifties, let me shower and then fed me – possibly too generously. Shall we say that he could talk for Britain, and perhaps needed to, since it turned out that he had not long been divorced. At the very point where he was opening up, and needed a sympathetic and alert listener, I found myself requiring a couple of giant matchsticks. In their absence my eyes simply insisted on shutting down for the night. The sofa was warm and restful, and I remained dead to the world for quite some time, before suddenly jolting back into reality. My impression was that the cascade of words had flowed unabated throughout, and that my sudden start went un-noticed by my host. A guilty look at my watch confirmed my secret worst fears – I had let him down for at least forty-five minutes, and lost any chance of giving my somewhat limited advice on that specific subject. As regards marriage my counsel is currently based more on theory than practice!

I know I shouldn't be too harsh on myself, but there was an obvious way out of this whole scenario. My host deserved to know just how tired I was. "Tell it how it is" comes to mind . . .

Say that again!

Some Scots I can understand reasonably well, with others I am aurally challenged. For me Peterhead, Fraserburgh, Glasgow, Dumfries are definite no-no's. Late one afternoon, following a twenty-mile slog I ended up with a delightful family, whose ten-year-old son plainly perceived me as the answer to all his prayers for someone to kick a football with. He gestured me outside and for the next hour bombarded me with conversation, blissfully unaware that I could make out less than ten per cent of what he was saying, though I supposed it to be English. I recognized that he was keen on wrestling, and also that I had found a friend for life – he followed me like Mary's little lamb.

Finally, too tired to continue kicking a ball, and extremely ready to answer the welcome call to eat, I beat a retreat to the kitchen. Mother was obviously aware that I found her son tricky to understand, and very kindly offered to act as an interpreter. Pretty much from that moment on she would repeat everything that he said. The problem was – I couldn't make out what she was saying either! You had to be there to appreciate the full irony of my situation. No need to repeat myself – the lesson is the same as the above.

The gypsy's home

As you can imagine, finding accommodation in the remoter parts of Scotland wasn't exactly easy. Before the sun rose one Tuesday morning, and whilst pessimistically surfing the net for options, Vincent happened across a highly impressive website. When phoning the pastor a bit later, he was surprised to find that the church membership roll contained only nine names. Nevertheless, there was an immediate positive response from the head honcho, and the very next Sunday his flock of nine was challenged to put up a random stranger from down south for a weekend. Frank's hand shot straight up, and the deal was settled there and then. It was only in the cold light of day that Frank remembered that his one bed-roomed bungalow had no space for visiting Sassenach rapscallions, not to mention having no spare bedding of any kind!

But I knew nothing of all this, as next Sunday Frank ushered me into a tired old caravan in his back yard. I was simply relieved to escape the slavering jaws of his fearsome Alsatian puppy, whose kennel was strategically and worryingly positioned on sentry duty immediately outside the caravan. Frank showed me a pretty OK place to lay my head, portable TV and all. It may have been my first caravan experience, but everything seemed fairly normal to me up to this point.

Later on, over dinner, the entire story began to unravel. Faced with his self-imposed accommodation conundrum, Frank had stumbled across a partly-furnished mobile gypsy home, apparently in the middle of nowhere, and definitely under urgent notice of police removal. Reasoning that he could make better use of it than them, he simply nabbed the unoccupied caravan right from under their noses. Having cleaned and cleared for my imminent arrival, he obviously relished the thought of being able to put future guests up in style.

Frank had a history of repeated detentions at Her Majesty's pleasure. In fact, he had only very recently renewed a former teenage commitment to Christ. Maybe he wasn't clear yet about the dos and don'ts of the faith, but he was refreshingly focused on the desire to serve others' needs above his own. What's that Bible verse about specks and planks?

CHAPTER 9

Silence Isn't Always Golden

Say what you see

I suppose at this point I had better join the thousands of other Christian writers from down the centuries who have addressed the subject of prayer. Let's face it; this whole adventure has been given the label of a prayer walk from day one. But I would hardly put myself in the same category as such greats as Andrew Murray, E.M. Bounds, G. Müller, R.A. Torrey, or erm, the Apostle Paul – to name but a few. In case you are feeling too impressed, be assured that I merely skimmed my way through most of these. But, in any case, I was all too aware throughout the project that reading and writing about prayer are no substitute for getting on and doing it! Sadly, all the background reading in the world would do you no good if you never actually uttered a word of prayer. You know what? I reckon I did more actual praying in those ten and a half months than in the whole previous twenty-five years of my life.

So, imagine for a moment that you were doing what I did. What ideas does it conjure up in your mind? Would you picture twenty-four draining hours of religious recitals, day-in, day-out for ten and a half months? Or perhaps receiving unwelcome lists from people you don't know for people you don't know – emergency 999 prayer calls for divine cat rescue? What about wondering endlessly whether or not you are even worthy to pray to the Almighty? Would you get stressed out

213

by deciding what most deserved your prayers – the future of our nation, or the bump on little Joey's head?

Well, all that was not my experience. It was far less formal than I had envisaged. To call something a prayer-walk implies a sense of demand, and produces twitchiness about implied expectation, but the reality was more like a comfortable daily relationship with a good friend. Long periods of being alone – with only God for company – taught me the habit of chatting to Him about everything I was thinking, feeling and doing, as I would if I were with my best mates.

Beforehand, I partly shared the popular opinion that there is no point in telling God about something of which He is already aware. Doesn't He know everything anyway? I'd even heard people say that God can read His own newspapers! But now it seems to me that the logical conclusion of such thinking is to stop praying altogether. Of course, in a technical sense, God doesn't *need* us to inform Him about everything that is going on. On the other hand, prayer in the form of *two-way*-communication is His idea, and I believe He loves it when we natter away to Him just for relationship's sake.

It became normal to share my feelings with God about everyday things. For example, I might twist my ankle a bit, whilst negotiating the side of a not so tricky ditch. Rather than simply saying, "Ouch, God, that hurt!" I would find myself going into detail with Him about it. He very soon heard not merely about the degree of pain it had caused me, but also my views on my own stupidity in taking insufficient care. Before I knew it, a prayer for instant miraculous healing would slide off my lips. I would wonder aloud with God whether His Son, Jesus, had ever done the same sort of thing. Did He tell His Father all about any occasional errors, like cutting a piece of wood too short, or the pain of a splinter?

Of course, you can't expect to be best friends with God overnight. Everything and anything could be strange to begin with. The same applies whenever you're getting to know somebody. But, once we trust more, we share more. Prayer is so relational in its very nature that it needs to be worked at as carefully as one might nourish any new friendship.

Close friends talk together about their true inner hopes and fears. If an individual has no one with whom to share on this level, then nine times out of ten that person will also be desperately lonely. Sometimes people never really cross the bridge of believing God desires such a degree of intimacy. Throughout the journey I was often questioned about whether I felt alone, and it is true that from time to time I did. But, for most of the walk I could truthfully deny it, because I wasn't travelling by myself. God was my soul-mate!

It goes without saying that I expected a fair bit of prayer support and back-up from home, but there was one aspect that surprised and deeply moved me – that was the kids! Many of the under-eights, with their parents' help, put maps on walls plus photos nearby of me in all my hiking gear, and daily moved pins around the maps to follow my progress. This not only reminded them to pray for me, but got them prompting their parents to do the same! At various times before setting out, I had made the tongue-in-cheek challenge to children in schools that they should inscribe my name on their tooth-brushes as an additional daily Gary-reminder. It amazed, and encouraged me, to see how many actually did. Anyway, among those of whom I know, I'd like to honour Jade, Ethan, Anna, Emily, Abby, Alice, Charlotte, Faith, Louise, Elie, the May boys and Simeon by giving them this mention here. Thank you!

I'm sure to miss out some of those who prayed regularly for me, so I'm sorry if I do. You will get your reward when you reach heaven. I really appreciated my mum who emailed me via my phone each day – often this would include prayers from her that were spot on. She kept a daily diary for every day of the walk which I have kept. Then there was Francoise who texted me more than once a week with words of encouragement and inspiration, Alison who received prophetic dreams and insights and phoned to share them, and Tony who faithfully ran a weekly prayer meeting – and would phone me up once a week for prayer needs. Also worth another mention in this context are Andy, Tom, Vincent, John, Jeremy, Cara, Squibbs, Trudy, the Bloomfield family, Sophie, Heather, Cyril and Margaret, Matt, Sikan, Luke, and Mel – each of whom frequently communicated with me. Without these faithful warriors, I am convinced that I would have quit before I'd started. God knows how much your intercessions helped me to carry on through the tough times. I now see every text or email you sent as part of your heart's prayer for me.

I would like to say with all my being that God does answer when we call, and I've seen it first hand. "God seems to do nothing except in response to our prayers." Don't ask me why or how, but I'm convinced that's the way it works. How many times have you been taught that God sometimes responds "Yes", other times "No", and still other times "Wait"?

I agree with that, but too many times we use it as an excuse to our unanswered requests. We stop short, believing that God has said "Wait", instead of pushing through. We back down to accepting it was a "No", get discouraged, doubt, and ultimately become bitter towards God. If only we could see deep into His heart, and hear His sweet words of "Yes and Amen", to any prayer that is in the name of His Son.

"Seek and you shall find, ask and you will receive, knock and the door will be opened unto you. If you ask anything in My Name it will be done for you." Sure, we are to make our requests with the right motives, but don't tangle yourself up examining your attitudes so much that you never get to pray. We have not because we ask not. Let God take care of why you are doing it, and whether it is right or not; our job is to pray. I have found that during real heartfelt prayer ungodly motives change anyway, as you tap into God. The more you draw close to the Master Potter, the more He will change you.

That's enough about what I think. It is time to read some answers for yourself. Hopefully it will stir and encourage your faith. It is your choice whether you believe these or not. But they are taken either from first-hand experience or from interviews that I did with various Christians, mostly hosts. I think they are genuine!

The old lady at the bus stop

There are times when God doesn't seem to be sounding too clear, whereas the voice of the enemy is loud and in your face. I remember walking past a bus stop in Wickford. No, don't worry! I wasn't about to flake off and take a bus ride further down the road, even though it was raining. I started to pass by, really annoyed to think that those passengers would do in thirty minutes what would take me all day. Standing in the queue was an elderly lady – and for some reason I felt my heart go out to her. At the same moment, a rather disturbing inner voice said, "Leave her there; she is not worth it – walk by!" But I knew it could not possibly be God. I didn't actually sense anything from Him, but I knew that He stood in direct contradiction to those words. I thought, "No, actually this lady might need someone, purely to chat to." So I stopped, and started chatting to her.

At first, the conversation was not too spiritual. In fact, we were talking about the weather and passing the time of day. Then, all of a sudden, she blurted out, "Do you know what the highlight of my day is?" I had no idea, but of course it was a rhetorical question. Without listening to my reply, she continued ... "Paying the milkman – it is the only time I ever get to talk to anyone!" The floodgates having opened, my new friend began to share in depth about her despair. What dumbfounded her most was that I just sat there and listened without either looking at my watch, or wanting to get away to the next appointment. I saw a tear run down her face; she could scarcely take it all in. It was time to tell this lonely sweetie about the man Jesus who would always be there for her. A smile began to spread over her face as she began to think that Someone special could be there for her at all times. I gave her a little tract, before she jumped on the bus, and poor old me continued trekking towards Maldon with her words reverberating in my head. "Thank you, you have made my day." What...? I had barely done anything except be there for someone.

Some churches grow quicker than others

Trevor and Susie are a great couple who started a church about three to four years ago. It began from scratch – that's zero – and was at one hundred and fifteen at the moment I stayed with them. I asked Trevor how they did evangelism, hoping to pick up some amazing strategy that we had been somehow missing all our lives. He said in a deadly serious yet graciously polite way: "We prayed them in!"

Trev then went on to tell me about strangers who would wander in on Sunday mornings and give their lives to Jesus off the back of the prayer meetings which underpinned everything their church did. They lived the gospel. In my short stay of a night and a morning their house always had people in as they shared, and gave advice to people on the fringes of faith.

Maybe we still have something to learn when it comes to complicated evangelism programmes. Try praying them in! How about this for a quote from one of those greats? As E.M. Bounds would say, "Faith and prayer select the things, and God commits Himself to do the very things which faith and persevering prayer nominate, and petition Him to accomplish" (*The Complete Works of E.M. Bounds on Prayer*, Baker Books, 1990).

I find that words spoken by God last much longer than those that we make up in our heads. In fact, because my memory is so poor these days, I find it a source of encouragement when words like these come back to me, because I wouldn't be able to make up the same thing again and again. By the way, I sound really old, but I'm still a spring chicken! I must have shared those words close on a hundred times, from home to home and church to church. Wherever they have been shared, it has also been impactive.

Our Dad is bigger than yours

Sorry this story is a bit graphic – but it is one that made a massive difference in the way I viewed the walk from this moment on. It happened whilst I was walking with a fella called Mark who had been joining me over a few days. We were heading for Bettyhill, which is a really beautiful spot by the way. Mark was an inspiration to be around – and his commitment to prayer was awesome. We had been praying for the nation together for quite some time when this vivid picture surfaced in my mind. It was of our enemy the devil, his hands clasped around Britain and laughing in a mocking fashion. But as we continued to pray his expression changed, his hands started to bleed, and his grip weakened as he came face to face with the God who answers prayer. It dawned on me from that day forth that this walk was not exclusively about a jolly-up, but it was about a warfare that is going on in the heavens. The more we pray, the more the devil loses grip!

Encouragement brings joy

Some days our job as Christians is to be channels of encouragement to bring others joy. I love to see a face light up, and a smile appear where there wasn't one. It takes more effort to frown than to smile, as I'm sure you know. To be an encourager is not that hard, but easily forgotten in a day where we tend to pick up on people's weaknesses, and continually talk about how to improve. Encouragement, I believe, is vital to the life of the church. Remove it, and you can almost kill an individual on the inside within a couple of years.

I loved that April morning when God decided to use me as His instrument to bring joy. I was totally unaware until the moment arrived. Having popped along to a morning prayer meeting with my host Sandra, I shared a verse that had been on my heart that morning about the mustard seed of faith being able to move mountains. Amongst those present was Anne, who became very excited as a radiant smile broke out across her face. She kept saying "I must tell my husband! I must tell my husband!" Completely unknown to me she was waiting for some confirmation, and I had said the exact words she was looking for. I walked with a buzz for the rest of that day, knowing that through God I had been able to bring a smile where there had been frowning uncertainty.

Is that a parrot?

I love the times where God speaks to you in your conscience, then seconds later someone else says exactly the same thing. I believe it is one way in which God shows Himself to be real. Of course you can never prove it to anyone else, and they might even think you are more than a touch crazy, but you know what the voice said deep down inside and there is no denying it. When it happens, it is one of those hair-standing-on-end moments.

I was walking with Phil, a new-found mate from one of the local churches in that area, when this voice went off inside me. "This place has a problem with ungodly gossip!" No sooner did it stop than Phil began to say the same words! Now, when this sort of thing happens, it fans into flame the desire to pray because you begin to sense you are touching something of God. The whole thing is not too complicated for God to do.

As a Christian, I believe God can read our thoughts. So all He needed to do was look into Phil's mind, and then communicate to me in advance what Phil was about to say. If you're a Christian, you know exactly what I'm talking about! It's so cool!

This has happened to me more times than I could mention, but I would like to share with you one other experience. I was in Dundee at a prayer meeting – following my day's walk – when John happened to read out the same Bible verse I had read myself that morning. "The Lord rejoices over us with singing" (see Zephaniah 3:17). Well, to know that God was doing that there and then could only inspire me to reach out to Him more. Out of all the verses in the Bible, one was chosen that I had read earlier. There must be more chance of me winning the National Lottery than of that happening.

We should care about the ring

After sitting down for a break when close to the Kyle of Lochalsh, I noticed an empty ring box on the floor beside me. God was trying to say something about marriage break-ups. People in the area were not worrying about the ring anymore – there were relational problems here. My job was to pray that marriages would be saved, and that God would restore the broken-ness and betrayal of human hearts.

Later on I met up with that day's hosts, who of course were totally unaware of what had happened to me earlier. Guess what? Before long, John started talking about relational problems in the area, which were apparently so big that John half-jokingly suggested that soon every possible combination would be exhausted, unless brothers and sisters started going out. I told John about what I had seen earlier and we prayed together, knowing that God had brought it to our attention.

God zooms in

Have you ever seen the *Truman Show*? It is a movie about a guy called Truman Burbank – who is the subject of a massive worldwide reality TV programme. But Truman doesn't even know that he is on it, let alone the central character. He is totally unaware that every Tom, Dick and Harry knows all his deepest secrets. Cameras are hidden absolutely everywhere he goes. It's the same with God. He can see our whole world at all times and can zoom in on any individual, at any given time. There were times when I felt Him panning in on me.

We all need God's mega pixel lens from time to time, to highlight the real picture of what is going on in our lives. A photo taken at a distance doesn't really show a great deal. But a close up – right down to those juicy blackheads on your face – can reveal a lot more. God can take an inside snapshot, and then reveal us, warts and all! He does this so we can see what we are really like, and then He gets on with the editing.

If you could have taken an image of me any week from Monday to Friday it would usually have revealed a genuinely God-focused committed prayer walker. I was really happy and fulfilled doing it on those days. But Saturdays were different – they've always been different! Saturday is my day, for chilling out with friends, unwinding, socialising, and basically doing not-God stuff. So every weekend the super focused lens would reveal another Gary grinding unwillingly along, preoccupied with self-pity. What I'm trying to say is – we can sometimes look pretty good to others from a distance, but God sees a close-up reality shot.

God looks after the young ones

Staying with my slightly freakier and creepier stories, I am convinced I heard a baby's cry more than once. At the time absolutely no-one was about – and no houses were in sight.

On both occasions, I'm sure it was God's way of reminding me to pray for the small ones in our nation. I vaguely remember a *Children in Need* programme on TV a couple of years back, involving Nigel from *Eastenders*. He quoted a figure of something like one in four where children suffer some form of sexual, or physical abuse in their life-time.

God doesn't want that, He loves kids. Jesus had a special place for them in His heart and on His knee. So, I found myself praying and crying for justice to come again in our land, as well as about abortion and its effects. After a while I sensed that something was going on in the area which needed immediate attention. My prayers became more intense and desperate – and then they eased as a police car shot past me at high speed with lights blazing. I knew that emergency response was the answer to the cry of a needy child somewhere.

God's banner of rescue

One morning I awoke and was unable to shake the word "rescue" from my mind. I pictured a banner with the letters extravagantly painted across it, with an edge of victory to each one. I think rescue and victory often go together. I was listening to my MP3 player at the time, and to my complete surprise the next song that came on was all about rescue and banners.

The next chain of events confirmed even more that it was right for me to be thinking about banners, and the word "rescue" and all that it means. I saw a random banner stuck in a bush. Coincidence? Maybe – or maybe not! That night, I got to watch a film all about rescue.

The same theme still carried on throughout the next day. My mum, who emailed me daily with words of encourage-ment, wrote about Daniel and his mates being saved by angels from the heat of the fiery furnace (Daniel 3:26). Finally Douglas, my host for that day, asked me to help hang a banner outside his church advertising Alpha. I told him everything that had built up to this crescendo over the last couple of days. We knew God wanted us to pray for the start of that Alpha course. I prayed with more certainty than normal, because of God's initiative in communicating His will.

Mustard seeds can move mountains

An idea began to surface in my mind about mustard seeds and my church back home. There is a Bible verse which says – if we have faith as small as a mustard seed – we can move a mountain. Firstly, I wanted to see how big a mustard seed was, then I wanted to buy a load and hand them out at church on my next home visit. Nobody had told me then that in Israel mustard seeds are different, and much, much smaller than ours! Anyway, it didn't really matter. The idea was for everyone to take a mustard seed as a symbol of a prayer requiring real faith – and they were to keep that small seed until the prayer was answered. Once that happened, they were to hand in the seed to a central pot, and join someone else who had yet to see their prayer answered. I came back home, shared the idea and handed out the seeds – one per person. Many have now handed in the prayer seed, having seen amazing answers to prayer. It is ironic that my own small seed still remains, as I was quite adventurous in my request. I hold that seed every time I pray for this certain thing.

Flint and more than one rainbow

One night, Nathaniel and I had been talking about God keeping His promises, and how there was a need not just to read about them, but to trust in them. We were both desperately needing some reassurance. As we walked towards Flint next day, we saw no fewer than four rainbows. I don't know whether you are familiar with the story of Noah and the ark, but in it God specifically uses a rainbow to act as proof that He will never again completely flood the earth. They are beautiful to look at, but are also there as a reminder that God is true to Himself – and that if He makes a promise He will never break it.

Busy roads can be lonely roads

The Bible tells us about two paths that exist, one of which each of us must choose. There is a narrow way to life which few find, the other is the wide road to destruction which many tread. I will let someone else argue about the theology of the verse, while I tell you about what I believe the paths are like to walk. Sorry for stating the obvious, but there are many people on the wide road, but most of them are focused on their own journeys – and finding satisfaction in that "Look out for number one!" mentality. So, despite the fact that there is so much hustle and bustle, it can be incredibly lonely there. Travellers keep stepping on each others' feet, and barging for position. It is easy to get lost although the road is wide – for there is no-one who knows the directions.

The narrow way is less busy, and harder to find. But once you are on it there is an altogether different feel. People are helping each other loads more – sometimes even at personal cost. When one falls down another picks them up and they walk on hand in hand for mutual support. Plenty of signposts indicate the right direction. The difference between a Christian and someone who doesn't believe is that the Christian has walked both paths, and knows which is better through conscious choice. The non-believer knows one road only, although the other option is always available.

The words that remained

Apparently the combined result of an excellent weekend and a deliberate lie-in was to open up my ears to God, because that

day I received what I believe was a word from Him, which
was going to stay with me as a recurring theme throughout
the entire walk, and even up to this day!

> "Blow away the cobwebs, and return to the things of
> old. Return to prayer in the homes, the breaking of
> bread in homes, and to the reading of the Scriptures
> together aloud in the homes. Return to the things of
> old, and you will see the very things you dream about,
> an unleashing of the power of God, the like of which
> you have never seen. Return to the things of old and
> blow away the cobwebs."

This whole story began in the context of my church family, so
it is only right to let some of them have the final words. In the
appendix that follows you will find their personalized
accounts of what it was like to experience life on the road
together or in the background making things happen. As you
will see, each one expresses a sense of excitement, fulfilment,
and a coming closer to God which really warmed my heart as
I read them.

But for now let us consider, and be stirred to follow the
ancient path. The fast lane of the twenty-first century compels
us towards a focus on gadgetry, and the latest methodology,
and an obsession with celebrity. Not to mention the distorted
philosophy of the workplace, whereby today's employee does
the equivalent of three jobs merely to satisfy someone's greed
somewhere, with a corresponding damage to all other aspects
of life. As a result too many of us have been forced to find our
identity mostly in our work.

On my walk I continually saw examples of families infected
with this winter bug. Even full-time Christian ministers,
whose jobs might seem on the surface to provide opportunities for peace and reflection, frequently mentioned the pain of

their disillusionment and frustration at feeling weighed down by the burden of ever-increasing expectation.

I am convinced that God has got something better, and that it lies in the prophetic word above. My passion is to see this vision blossom into reality. So let's recognize the call of spring, the dawning of a new season and draw a sharp intake of breath strong enough to blast away the most persistent cobweb of substandard living.

I really believe this is close to what Jesus meant when he said,

> *"The thief comes only to steal and kill and destroy; I have come that they may have life and have it to the full."* (John 10:10)

Appendix

God's alongsiders

There is a great divide between people who say they will do something, but never get round to really doing it, and those who show up, and get their feet blistered, as it were. I'm so glad to say that there were only a few who bigged themselves up, and then never arrived – most of my closest friends actually kept their word and walked with me. The amount of effort that went into travel plans, sorting work schedules, getting fit enough to walk at least 225,000 metres in a single day must have been immense. Then there would have been the many Radox muscle-soothed baths required afterwards to pacify those dead legs and indignant feet. I really appreciate all those who paid the price, and I'm very grateful to have heard back from so many of you that it really was all that you wanted it to be.

It is a paradox that at the same time as my heart longed to have friends walking with me, I also knew how important it was to be free to give myself totally into the vision, and that meant walking alone a lot of the time. If God had wanted me to have companions all the way then He would have prepared my heart differently. But when they came it was great! If I include the occasional host who walked with me, it worked out that about once in every four days someone joined me. Looking back, that was about the right proportion.

The ages and levels of fitness of those who walked with me varied enormously from four to eighty-two, male and female. Despite all we hear today about the equality of the sexes, sadly there was less than a ten per cent show from the more fragile members of the species. Or was it that over such a short period of absence my charm had lost its power to draw?! Were they just short of time because they were so busy doing all the praying in the background?

However that may be, I feel that it is right to offer my family and friends their moment of literary fame – if that is how you describe being able to contribute to my book! Yes, and even the ladies!

Minehead

Gary had been walking for quite a few months when I joined him near Minehead for a two day stint. I was really looking forward to our time together but – human nature being what it is – I started by focusing in on myself. Would I find the place, or get lost? What about my car? Will I be fit enough to keep up? The first night was in a B & B with an excellent breakfast. (Food is always high on my list of priorities!) As we left our excellent Christian hosts we prayed that the Lord would open up opportunities for us to pray for people. Gary was keen for me to feel comfortable and useful, so he asked in what way I felt gifted to minister. I have always been a practical person, willing to "get my hands dirty" – so that is what I said. As Gary told me about some of the things that had happened to him, I felt our relationship became closer.

The terrain was very hilly and the walk was tiring, but the scenery was so beautiful it made up for any physical discomfort. Being keen on bird watching, I was delighted to see a buzzard, although the first few times we chased after them they turned out to be crows! This is reminiscent of the Christian walk; sometimes we have to chase a few crows before we find the greater reward. We had extremes of weather, from very wet and blustery to warm sunshine. This combination also bore its own rewards. Walking up a narrow lane with woods on our right, you could see a rainbow through the trees. It appeared to hit the ground only a few yards away. On another occasion, we were looking out over the Severn estuary, and we saw a rainbow arching over South Wales. We had just been praying for Wales, so it was a visible sign of encouragement. Opportunities arose for us to pray with people in a Christian bookshop, different churches, and with our Christian hosts. It was good to hear about other people's ministries, and what God is doing in their area.

On the second day, we were approaching a Christian retreat. We knocked on the door of the gatehouse, which was answered by a little child, who announced that mummy was having a bath. We asked the child to tell mummy that we were two Christians, and we were praying for her. Later on, at the retreat, we learned that the house and its occupants were completely unconnected. We did wonder if we would be mentioned on the local news as two men to be wary of!

Following a large pub lunch, we were praying again for a way to serve someone. We saw two guys up ahead. They were lost, and we were going in the same direction as they needed to go, so we walked with them. We told them about the Lord and carried some of their belongings. They were very interested in Gary's walk. It turned out we were staying in the same guest house.

As we walked, Gary told me about a book he had been reading, *Wild at Heart*, by John Eldridge. It had blessed Gary so much that he bought me a copy. I am not very fond of reading, but this captivated me, and has helped me to focus more on God. I believe the Lord used both Gary and this book to speak to me about going to Rwanda. I had been asking Him to give me a new vision for my life. I did not know, but my wife had been praying that I would want to go with her next time she travelled there. In June 2006, I found myself on a plane to Rwanda with my wife and a mission team which was led by Gary!

Those two days with him were like an oasis in the desert, which brought Gary and me closer together, but more importantly closer to my Lord.

Peter Hall

Prayer supporter

It was a great privilege to be part of Gary's "support team", by running a Tuesday lunchtime prayer meeting during most of the period of the walk.

My regular routine was to contact Gary by phone every Tuesday morning, with road-map to hand, and first of all establish exactly where he was, what the weather was like, and how he was feeling that particular day.

It was good to hear his voice, to learn first-hand what God was doing through him, and to be informed about the opportunities that were facing Gary on the day in question.

I was encouraged by those who came to join in prayer for Gary. Our numbers were never particularly large, but this was understandable considering the time of day we met. Some faithful souls joined me practically every Tuesday!

Did God ever answer our prayer requests? Yes, He did, and three instances may illustrate this . . .

First, Gary developed painful blisters early on. But, at exactly the right time, he found himself due to stay with a chiropodist, who dealt effectively with his problem!

Secondly, when Gary eventually arrived in Scotland, we prayed that he would understand the local dialect. In time, he did!

Thirdly, we often prayed that the weather would be favourable for Gary when walking. Josie, one of our "regulars", frequently prayed specifically, "Lord, may it rain in front of

Gary, and behind him, but not *on* him!" That request was answered more than once.

There were other answers to prayer, but the three mentioned above come specifically to mind.

Tony Coombe

North Somercotes

I was keen to walk with Gary from the moment I heard he was doing the walk, and yet more so when he came to Grimsby! This is because it is where I grew up and became a Christian ... Gary was to stay with my Auntie and Uncle ... I had no idea what they would think of Gary's walk, but I was sure they would all get on, as they share a love for good food and sport on TV!

Louise and I drove the two-hour journey from Derby to North Somercotes, not knowing what to expect ... part of me thought it would be little more than a nice chat and stroll, with a bit of praying. But I hoped it would be more, that we would see God do and say something amazing!

I met up with Gary, and his hosts had clearly enjoyed his company! We set out and walked alongside the road for a short distance. Almost immediately after leaving the road onto the footpath, Gary had spotted somebody and was telling him about the walk. A moment later we were invited in for a cup of tea, had a good chat and were soon praying for John Wilson and his sick relation. It seemed like we were a real encouragement to John, a Christian from a very small, ageing church, and that God had brought the meeting about! Gary had also clearly learned not to turn down biscuits!

We carried on along footpaths, through fields of crops. The landscape was flat. It felt like we were quite a way inland, with no sign of the coast, but this was because of the adjacent army bombing range, which we decided it best not to walk through!

We came to a village, and were walking alongside the road, when somebody stopped to ask me for directions. Before I had a chance to say anything, Gary was inputting the request into his satnav computer. This gave us a chance to talk about the walk ... it was a blatant divine appointment! The lady's daughter had become a Christian that week, and she had been thinking a lot about it. After a bit of persuasion from Gary, she even acknowledged it as a sign from God. I was so impressed with the way Gary didn't beat about the bush, and how he clearly and concisely witnessed to these strangers. In fact, Gary appeared to take it that any person in our path had been put there by God for him to talk to. This was inspiring, exciting, and totally refreshing, and I'm sure it got a lot of people thinking.

Spending so much time talking and walking with Gary made me miss the people I know in Folkestone! It had been a long time since God had talked specifically about where I lived and what I was doing, and on a recent visit to Kent I had such a lovely time and was made so welcome. I went away wondering if I should go back there! Well, God wasn't going to keep quiet for long, we went into the pub in Marshchapel [*I think*], and met a regular who was a retired taxi driver from Derby. He specifically knew my house, which was quite amazing! We ordered our food, sat down, and carried on talking, specifically about where I should be, and at that moment I looked up. There, next to Gary's head, was a framed picture of Derbyshire ... and looking around the pub, it was the one place represented. I knew so clearly that God had spoken, and to be honest, that time was a real turning point in my feeling of belonging in Derby.

The walk continued with prayer, conversation and fun. We came to a ditch, and initially couldn't find a crossing! When we did, we still decided to jump it for a laugh! This was great fun, so much so we jumped the next ditch (which was half as wide again), despite finding a crossing! As we continued across the next field, we came across the mother of all ditches – twice as wide as the previous one. We really didn't want to jump, but in the end submitted, and jumped. Gary went first, and was wet up to the knees after only getting three-quarters of the way. I went and got a boot-full of water too! This was great!

The walk continued, with the Holy Spirit leading our prayers. There was to be another amazing divine appointment. Gary deliberately took a wrong turn, led by God, and moments later stopped a chap walking the other way. Initially, this guy looked worried, but soon warmed to us. He was a trainer of missionaries, he had a son called Gary, and his name was Colin Lamb! Our Gary Lamb felt led to give him some money. So it was mind-blowing, when a moment after this Colin said that he had actually gone out that day to pray for provision from God, and this was the result.

The rest of the day's walk was great, finishing in Grimsby. Gary got on so well with my family, who still ask about him now. This was the most inspiring day of 2005 for me. God's presence was just so obviously with the walk, and it is my testimony that this changed and inspired those who walked with Gary!

James Brown

Exeter

Walking with Gary was a valuable experience. The reality is that we have a responsibility to pray for our nation, and to pray purposefully for people in their current circumstances. My time spent with Gary highlighted the effectiveness of encouraging and praying for people we don't even know. Who knows what effect our prayers and encouragements had on the couple who agreed to answer questions about their belief in God; or the two old gentlemen walking on the sea front who were encouraged by our prayers asking God for healing; or the man in the pub who gave us "drinks on the house" after we told him Gary was prayer walking around Britain; the man at the station who let us pray for him; the vicar whose door we knocked on and later prayed for in relation to the youth in his church; the walkers we helped with directions and gave a booklet to about what Jesus had done for them? We make a difference through what we do.

Tom Hydes

Swansea

It all started with Joshua hearing about the possibility of going to spend a day with Gary on the prayer walk, to which he said – "Yes . . . when?" I realized there was no way out, and started planning . . . November? The Gower, where I was a local lad? Game on!

Ignoring the after-effects of an ulcerated throat, Josh and I drive down towards Port Eynon on Friday through some really heavy rain. As we think of him battling through, our hearts are . . . to be with Gary and encourage him . . . to add our weight to prayers for the locality . . . to witness to people . . . to play our part in opening up the area to the power of God. We are excited!

God leads us straight to the secure parking area, in an attended locked old bus depot, right next to the new bus station, and we take the precaution of eating a MacDonalds! Nearly dark now, onto the bus and out into Gower. A Welsh lady speaks to the driver, heaves herself up, and flops into the luggage rack, where she remains for the duration. We get off at Penmaen, but find that the directions aren't too good, so we knock on a door to ask for Nicholaston House – never heard of it! Dark, windy, raining . . . mobile phone to the house . . . answerphone message – oh, dear! But someone picks up and comes for us . . . we have got off one stop too early! We arrive and meet up with Gazza!

We share a room. All the rooms have names – Peace, Comfort, Joy – ours was Faith! Very comfortable accommodation.

We then get news that a meal is being prepared – well, who needs MacDonalds anyway? Josh assures me he will still eat it. I am less sure ... but we do! Relax in lounge watching Wales vs Fiji, a good running game. Wales win – even better. Look at Gary's photos on his digital – some amazing shots.

Bed at approx 10.15 plus late night cup of char. Overnight wind howling, heavy rain, leaking gutter, creaky beds, toilet trips, but we all get some sleep! What will tomorrow bring?

Josh wakes at seven, get him to make Gary (and me) a cup of tea. Use Gideon Bible in room. Eat enormous cooked breakfast as we look out over Oxwich Bay. Hilarious topic – most embarrassing toilet moments – sorry, no details! Set off at 9.15 a.m. Down through Crawley Woods onto Oxwich Bay, cross sands to Tor Bay, nip around point over mussel beds before tide comes in. Into Three Cliffs Bay, not possible to cross stream, swollen by heavy rain. Follow river into stepping stones, raining, huge sandbanks, Gary and Josh having fun. Cross Pennard Pill back down to three cliffs and up small cliff over to Pobbles Bay. Meet first punters, who can't think of anything to pray for, so Josh prays for their injured dog instead. Up cliff to Pennard, several chats, wild dogs with owner bit of a hazard, prayed anyway. One atheist, one all-roads-lead-to-God, lots of hellos etc., lane to Pwll Du past Hunts Farm, Gower man who thinks Gower is the Promised Land, and how dare we miss Rhossili? Muddy path drops down to Pwll Du bay, inaccessible to cars and most sensible people. Skies clearing.

I tell Gary of old family links to this place, middle-of-nowhere cottages, etc., so he says, "Right, let's knock on some doors." Only a few, so we do, and Kamarl (southern Asian guy who owns house, plus software company, etc.) pops his head out! I mention family connections here. "Yes, I know of John Timothy," he says, and asks us in for a welcome cup of tea!

Two friends there, Alan Davies and Colin Lucas. Am related to Alan via Mary Webborn, and Colin knows my Grandpa's cousin, Uncle George Webborn, the carpenter! Seems Webborns were landed gentry in the past etc. etc. – so what happened? It's a small world, when you're a Webborn! Gary witnesses and plays snooker. Tales of smugglers and wreckers at Pwll Du, candles on cows' horns luring ships to their doom – no relation, I hope! They ask if we are going to the "Leap of Faith", high precipitous pathway round Caswell Head, with 100 foot sheer drop. Yes, we are, since the wind has dropped. Eventually up to Tichbourne, take note of one of Catherine Zeta Jones's residences, past Auntie Rose's by the farm, down to Park Avenue. Sit by fire with Auntie Margie, egg sand-wiches, sponge cake and tea – 4.5 miles to Swansea, round the bay on the flat, Gary measures it on his hand-held GPS.

Point out Devon Place, where I was born; also Mumbles Christadelphian hall, where I spent a lot of time growing up. Doors are open, can see Auntie Glenys. Tap her shoulder, ask if she knows who I am. She says, "No!" It's been a few years, never mind. She finally realizes; hope she recovers soon!

Loads of people now out walking, jogging etc. We begin giving words of encouragement and blessing to people. Josh likewise starts to flex his spiritual muscle, prays for an old man on a scooter who thanks him, and for some young lads on a climbing frame. Gary prays for deaf man walking alone, I give word of encouragement and challenge to a bearded cyclist.

Legs start to really hurt now, same with Josh. Gary prays for a lady who we think was a witch! Targeting where car is parked – now in sight, praise God! There is a pub right next to where car is parked; we go in to watch the England vs Argentina game 3:2. English, Irish and Welsh in the pub, a heady mix, plus Welsh ladies intent on talking to us. Try to let Gary watch the footie and I tackle them head on! Big lady swearing like a trooper before I moved over. While I talk, the Holy Spirit noticeably silences this, and she starts sharing about her upbringing in Sunday school. God strongly on her case. I know she is convicted, but at the same time God is forgiving her. Apparently her name is Gwyneth Ogwyn (or something) Davies, or god for short. Other lady suffering from recent rejection, blaming God for everything. Tell her God is her friend and she can talk to Him. Alcohol begins to cut in, numbing her senses, and she accepts prayer in the pub just before it does. May she have one Holy Hangover . . . !

Look at what God can do in one day and fifteen miles! If you have a particular area on your heart, pray into it and what you should do. God will use your faith to break down barriers. You never know, you may find yourself having to prayer walk, too!

Phil Webborn

Hastings

I woke with great excitement looking forward to my walk with Gary. While praying, I felt led to print off John 3:16 in different translations, including French, in case of any opportunities I might encounter. I knew I would be travelling on a school bus, so being the first person upstairs, I laid John 3:16 on random seats while praying.

During the journey, as teenagers boarded the bus, I had great fun listening to them trying to decipher the French version. I had placed a Scripture verse on the seat adjacent to me, which a young lady read then put in her bag. She was smiling as she got off the bus. It was a blessed start to the day.

When I met Gary, he looked fit and well. I was so pleased to see him. As we walked through Hastings, we popped into a church and prayed. There were two electricians working and Gary spoke briefly to them. Before leaving the building, we wrote prayer requests putting them in a prayer basket. We also prayed for needs already there. During our walk, Gary challenged me on healing, asking why I thought we don't see instantaneous healings as Jesus did. Shortly afterwards, we met two elderly ladies looking for a place to eat. We directed them to where we were about to lunch. Gary helped one of them as she had trouble walking, including an ulcerated leg. The other lady had a blind stick. Gary prodded me to pray for them. After our meal, and before leaving, I plucked up courage and prayed for them both. Sadly there was no obvious sign of any change. Once out of the pub, we got talking, and Gary dared me to return and ask the lady to remove the bandage on her leg, to see if there was a change. Although I wanted to, I didn't. I chickened out! Why? Well, what if I raised her hopes, and nothing happened? And would I feel embarrassed in a pub-load of people? I came to the conclusion that my faith level was pretty poor. I know Jesus heals, so I had prayed – why then didn't I expect Him to show up? A question I need to ask myself.

We continued our walk praying for various people.

The weather was beautiful, the journey very hilly. I was surprised I made it, but God wasn't. He ordained it before the beginning of time. Well done, Gary, it was a great pleasure walking with you! I enjoyed the day immensely. Thanks for going at my pace, you are an ace.

Mum (aged ... I am not allowed to tell you!)

Littlehampton

I had imagined that it would be at a more dramatic location – possibly John O'Groats, the Isle of Skye or Land's End? But Gary's progress had been such that – if I was to keep my promise of joining him for a day on his walk – it was now, or never! And so I found myself on a train pulling into Bognor Regis station, on an overcast day in February. There was Gary, looking healthy and raring to go, with a substantial pack on his back. Fortunately, I had chosen one of his shortest days of walking, a gentle eight-mile stroll to Littlehampton.

Having reached the seafront, we headed eastwards, stopping to pray as we were prompted by what we saw. Before long we passed Butlin's, with a group of young people coming out, and felt constrained to pray for it and those that visited and worked there. We saw a sign that simply said "France" pointing out to sea, causing us to halt and pray for that nation, and those we knew living and working there. The Royal Standard flying incongruously over a seafront house made us smile, and then pray, as we remembered the Royal Family and others in positions of authority and influence.

Pedestrians were few and far between, but was it coincidence that we met a Hungarian lady in her eighties who told us her life story? Imprisoned under Hitler and Stalin, she had lived for many years in the UK. Yet, despite her past, there was a germ of faith and we were able to pray with her as she went on her way.

Lunch (lasagne, I recall!) and a discussion at the bar of a local pub followed a visit to a small church. Having prayed inside and met the cleaners, we walked through the graveyard. When reading the headstones, we were reminded of the lives, struggles tragedies and victories of many people unknown to us, yet who were known, loved and valued by our heavenly Father.

After lunch there were even fewer people around, as we walked along alternating silence, discussion (from football to healing, and everything in between!) and prayer. By early afternoon we reached Littlehampton, heading straight for churches identified on the map. The first was vast, impenetrable, locked securely and with no way in. The second was smaller, but still locked, with no way in. However, a sign directed us to the manse next door where we met the minister. He was delighted to share, prayed with and for us, and requested intercession for a major inter-church event to be held at the Bognor Butlin's the following week.

After a brief sojourn watching the Rugby International in a

pub in Littlehampton, we concluded our day together. As Gary marched off to meet his host for the night, I returned to my car, reflecting that for just one day I had been able to create time to watch, listen, share and pray. Why do I not do this more often?

Jeremy Russell

Lowestoft

This was the first time I was to walk with Gary and was looking forward to catching up with him, after following the blogs for some time. We were booked in to stay with relatives from people in our church, and after a three-hour drive I was able to find the address. I found Gary recovering from bad blisters that week and gave him the new shoe liners for his boots (worn out after only two months!). We had a time of relaxing and getting to know his hosts for that evening and breaking down the barriers of being "weird" Christians!

The next morning, we started out after polishing off a nice cooked breakfast. It was raining and I felt a little apprehensive about the distance ahead, not having done much practice. Gary admitted that the planned route was actually one of his longest yet; we managed to get a short lift with his host to a location slightly round the coast – after agreeing to go and see his work place. We stopped at the telephone exchange and were shown around (I have never seen so many cables!). Our host (non-Christian) proudly introduced us to his work colleagues, and said a little about what Gary was doing. We were able to pray for his colleague who was recovering from cancer. Moving swiftly on, we started walking towards Norwich, stopping in villages on the way through the Norfolk Broads, and praying for the church congregations. I remember well standing on top of a village church tower (the tallest thing for miles) taking in the view and worshipping God, being able to appreciate God's creation. We also met some

Quakers at the top of the tower and had a brief discussion about the walk and their beliefs. We continued to walk, praying and chatting with people as we went, and also praying for houses and villages as we felt led. It was good to catch up with Gary and amazing how very heavy his backpack actually was. I went home feeling physically tired but spiritually renewed, Gary's walk was faith in action.

Tim Burgess

Golspie

This was the second time I was to walk with Gary. Emma (my wife) and I were due to be visiting Inverness on holiday the very time Gary was in that part of the country. One thing that amazed me was how that God looked after all the details, such as transport! We were able to offer Gary a lift home for his scheduled return to Kent. We started walking with Gary from a station near Golspie on the east coast of the Highlands. The scenery there is unbelievable in beauty but also very steep. People, along with houses, were few and far between, but we were able to enjoy each other's company and pray for the young people at home. We eventually came to a town called Brora and set off for the station – our method of returning back to our car. We stopped by at a small hotel to get a drink, and started chatting to the barmaid. She informed us without prompting that there were actually two stations in Brora and that the train only stopped at one of them! Maybe it was God's timing as it certainly helped us, since trains were few and far between in Brora. The 5 p.m. train was the last one before 8 a.m. the next morning! After a long day, we caught the train back to our car and headed to Helmsdale. We were impacted by Gary's unyielding enthusiasm to meet new people and share a little about God, in which ever way possible. "Accidents happen for a reason!" was the motto.

Tim and Emma Burgess

Hi Gazza,
It was good walking with you. We prayed for a lot of people,
and God was really there. It was amazing!

Thanx for adding me to the book.

From Sam (aged 14)

Holbeach

Walking with Gary was a great experience. He was actually
doing what God had wanted him to. I was able to see that
"hands on" and share in his journey. We met up the day
before and stayed overnight with a lovely American couple
who had moved to the UK on mission. They made us feel
really welcome in their home. Gary slept in the most
impressive four-poster bed I think I've ever seen!

We started the day with prayer, asking for opportunities to
meet and share with people.

Gary had our route to Holbeach well worked out, and we
set off in bright sunshine. We were walking in Norfolk, so the
land was nice and flat, no hills! Our journey took us mainly
through small villages.

It was a day of visiting and exploring churches, five or six I
think, and an opportunity for us to both rest, and to just enjoy
each other's company.

It was a day walking along and praising God for all that He
has created. It was a day walking along praising God, singing
songs, and listening to worship music. As we walked, we prayed
for the surrounding area, the communities we walked through
and passed, and an opportunity to meet people. We did seem
to attract attention (mainly, I think, due to the size of Gary's
rucksack!). Many people stopped to ask, "Where are you
going?" and "Why are you walking here?" Which was great!

The real highlight of the day was when we were walking
past the house of this elderly man. He was outside mowing his
front lawn, and as soon as we walked past he stopped the

mower, and said "Hello!" He looked unsettled, and told us there and then that he was going into hospital to have an exploratory operation, and that he was worried about it. We asked if it was OK for us to pray for him. He said he was not a Christian, but would really like that. We spent a few minutes standing in this complete stranger's front garden, with our arms around him, praying for healing and peace of mind. I think we left him feeling less anxious, that he was not alone and that God loved him. That moment confirmed to me that prayer can and does make a difference in people's lives.

Roger Hext

Fort William

I joined Gary in Fort William, Scotland. My journey up was quite spectacular. The train from Glasgow wound around the foot of the mountains, gradually creeping up to some open areas of land used for sheep farming. The railway line would have been quite a feat of engineering when built, and shows what we humans are capable of. However, the views of the valleys, lochs and mountains all around showed what an engineer our Creator is! "Magnificent" does not describe what I saw. Words fail me.

We prayer-walked around Fort William visiting as many places as possible. Whilst travelling on a boat to see Seal Island, we chatted to several people, but still Francis lives on in my memory today. An unassuming Welsh man on a journey to find something ... but not sure what! The weather that day was very Scottish, gloomy and wet. As I stood looking out over the loch from the boat, the clouds parted, and a ray of sun shone through, as if to say, "Here I am." That was it. I believe God spoke to me and told me to reassure Francis that He loves him, and that he was to pray, and God would reveal Himself. Ahhh! Now I've got to go and speak these words to a man I hardly know! Well, I suppose I probably won't see him again, and he'll just remember me as the mad Kentish man. But, perhaps he will remember the mad Kentish man that God spoke to that day, and it changed his life? Maybe he will find what he is looking for. To take this step of faith and trust God may indeed have changed Francis' life. I know it changed mine.

Whilst walking across the mountains to Glencoe, we stopped at the top of one. With the help of Gary's MP3 player we worshipped. I have never felt so free in worship as I did that day – out of tune, and almost shouting, we sang out to our God. There were no barriers, no restraints, nothing that was going to get in the way, not even the sore feet!

Both times I spent with Gary were fun, exciting and challenging, breaking through the limitations we set on ourselves. It was great to see my son and nephew pushing past those barriers, as they asked people on the street if they needed prayer, or to talk. It was a very special, encouraging time for me. Gary is a man with a big heart, and time for all, a gift that is rare today.

Chris Buck

A walk with God

A wonder of creation to behold
A search for riches, yet untold.
Black to white, darkness to light,
A pathway laden with misery and pain.
Horizons of hope and heavenly gain.
Tapes of foreboding, curses of doom,
Milky shadows of Satan's gloom.
Ancient messages in abject verse,
Prayer to withstand our enemy's curse.
Out of this darkness, back to the fold.
A destiny of righteousness,
A sanctuary of gold!

Jeremy Freemam

Gadgets man

Well, what can I say? It's a good job God doesn't depend on GPS (satellite navigation) to guide us. I suppose my main involvement started when Gary asked me for my so-called technical experience to help set up his new "toy", which was going to help speed him around the UK without getting him lost at his first junction in Folkestone. I'm not particularly technical, but like a challenge, and if worst comes to worst (seeing as I work in an IT department) I generally "know a man who could". Like all good gadgets, I think it lasted about two weeks before the thing went wrong, and I needed to make a speedy trip up to Gary's current abode to try and fix the system. I think that between the four of us (Gary, Luke Yates, myself and God) we muddled through – well, three out of the four of us are capable of getting muddled. The wonders of technology were up and working again within a couple of hours.

The hours spent loading the maps before Gary departed on his walk were well worth it, even though we had a couple of initial blips. It worked well, and mostly kept Gary out of trouble, which is a miracle in itself! Gary seemed chuffed with his new toy, choosing to use it around the wilds of Folkestone before he went ... purely to test it, of course! His disappointment that the pubs and Little Chef restaurants did not appear to be plotted on the maps were soon forgotten – I recall that one of his earliest updates listed the large number of "fry-ups" kindly provided by his many hosts.

I joined Gary on one leg of his journey, as he was about to discover the wonders of Hartlepool. After a superb night in one of the local B & Bs we came to pay, only to encounter the small issue that they took cash exclusively, and all we had on us was plastic. I remember the owner turning to us and saying we need not worry, we could post the money when we got home ... very unusual. God was certainly with us that day, or maybe Gary had a very trustworthy face ... or perhaps both! Before heading on our way, we found a local cash machine to pay our debt.

For me, the walk was something of a new experience. I'd been on prayer walks before, but it was the interaction with people that made this one for me. We were really "out in the field", praying way beyond my comfort zone at least. I came away on a "high", knowing that I was where God had wanted me to be, and that He has used us to touch the lives of several through word or deed.

John Rawlings

Gadgets again

When I was growing up, I loved spy films. In fact, I still do – and it wasn't the "saving the world stuff", though that was quite appealing. Nor was it the grisly deaths, caused by sharks, volcanoes or bowler hats. It certainly wasn't – and still isn't – the glamorous lifestyle, the flash cars or the beautiful women. I drive a Mini – you can't get more flash than that – and I have a very beautiful woman – my wife Claire. So I'm sorted in that respect, thanks.

No – the thing I love about spy films, more than anything else, is the gadgets.

Like the signet ring, that can fire a laser beam that can cut through prison bars. Or, perhaps, the shoe that contains a small tracking device, a change of clothes and a bottle of lemonade in its heel. Or the wrist watch, that's also a toaster as well as an espresso coffee machine.

Yes indeed – as an IT "geek" – it goes without saying that I love gadgets. I read about them and I play with them whenever I can.

So when Gary approached me to support his walk with my IT skills, I instantly thought to myself, *"Yes!* I'm going to be a *boffin."* I would become the guy behind the scenes who toils away beneath the city in his laboratory, wearing a white coat and supplying the special agent with the amazing gadgets that inevitably save the day.

Well, I certainly wasn't disappointed – there were no end of gadgets on Gary's walk – ones that I had the privilege of researching, testing and eventually handing over to him. (Sometimes quite reluctantly I admit!)

We had solar panel batteries, Sat-nav gizmos . . . you name it.

But – best of all – really cool, state-of-the-art computer software, sitting behind the scenes powering Gary's Prayer Walk Site! Which I got to write.

Gary's website needed what was – for me – a totally new idea. He wanted to be able to update his website whilst he was walking around Britain, and sometimes there wouldn't be a computer where he could sit and access the site. So we needed to do it using a specially-written website and an equally special mobile phone, which was one of my favourite "Gary Gadgets".

When I first showed Gary the phone, I almost found myself saying, "Now pay attention, Agent Lamb. It looks like an ordinary phone, but if you fold it out, it turns into a miniature keyboard!" Somehow I refrained . . .

The plan was that Gary would access a special page on his website, and this would allow him to type into his "blog" (an online diary that other people can read). As soon as he was done, the writing would be up on his website for all to see. Some days it worked great. Other days it really didn't.

Every now and again the system broke completely, and I'd get a phone call from Gary, at the top of some mountain or in the middle of a wood. So I'd go to my computer and try to work out what had gone wrong. On each occasion, with prayer from both ends (and a lot of patience from Gary's), we managed to get it working again.

Amazingly, it turned out that – for me – the best thing about this whole experience wasn't the gadgets.

When I look back, the thing I appreciate most is that I got

the chance to serve a really good bloke who simply had a call from God, and who was obedient to it. God called me to be involved too, and to be who He made me to be, in order to serve Gary, and to further God's kingdom. Plus I got to know Gary a whole lot better as a friend, and it was a tremendous honour to share in his journey every single day. Some days I read the blog, other days I got sent a text, or a photo, and on a few I had the privilege of seeing a video clip from the top of a mountain, or when he was admiring the scenery as he was walking along the coast. These were always breathtaking and blessed me immensely.

And I soon realized (especially when they went wrong) that Gary didn't *need* the gadgets. They were merely "nice to have" things. He just needed to keep walking with God, and to keep being obedient. As do we all.

Luke Yates

King's Lynn

It was a bit of a shock to find Gary obsessed with a new, portable idol, otherwise known as his SatNav GPS. This technological deity, which could be very forceful about commanding the route for each day, sadly lacked discernment regarding disused footpaths or blocked access points. My best friend and wife, Julie, will confirm if asked that my once OK memory is now more fragile than Gary's – and that is saying something! But I recall, as if it were yesterday, the April Wednesday when his hand-held god blatantly misled us. We woke up to it only on finding ourselves at the far side of a wood, surrounded by lakes and fences.

In such circumstances, as village-boy Vincent still remembered from the misty days of boyhood, it is vital to be totally flat in the grass when rolling, no matter how much it damages the pride. As a result, I emerged first on the other side of the obstacle, soaked but unscathed. The Lamb humility, usually of a high order, resisted the idea of prostrating himself so fully, and his kit came out slightly second-best in a duel with a couple of rusty spikes. I ought, of course, to have wept with those who weep! But I felt a little smug having showed the experienced walker how it was done!

All of which pales into absolute insignificance, by comparison with the unforgettable God-moments of the following day. We talked to Him about spending less time on Boy Scout manoeuvres and more on finding His contacts for the day. Gary was getting used to what to ask for, and at his suggestion we sought (and got) a "picture" of what we were to look for. I kid you not, this actually happened. It was a bright spring day but somewhere, we believed, we were to find a house with an outside light and an open door, where we would bring hope and encouragement. Well, the miles passed, and the original confidence that we had actually heard from God began to be challenged. Eventually we found ourselves in what Gary's GPS uncompromisingly declared to be the last bit of human habitation before we would need to cross some seven miles of open country and reach King's Lynn. It was one of those narrow, straggly villages, and all too soon we were obviously coming to the end of the single street. Then, from nowhere, we saw a lady with a dog in tow. We asked her if she knew where we could get some water-supplies. She pointed to almost the last house in sight, and led us there, promising to help. We were to have a great conversation, and to leave in the certainty that God had directed us that day specifically to bless her. And what sights greeted us, as we walked up the path? Yes, an outside light and an open door! It is an amazing sensation to realize that the God of the universe interests Himself in our doings so personally and supernaturally. I have always been a bit of a slow learner, and these two days with Gary (the first of a number of visits I would make) are milestones in my own journey of learning to listen to God.

Vincent Oliver

Big Boss Man

"Vision is spawned by faith, sustained by hope, sparked by imagination and strengthened by enthusiasm. It is greater than sight, deeper than a dream, broader than an idea. Vision encompasses vast vistas outside the realm of the predictable, the safe and the unexpected."

(Charles Swindoll)

I have lost track of how many people have come, at various times, to tell me about something they intend to do. I have to confess that the thought in my heart has usually been, "We'll just wait and see!"

When Gary first shared his early thoughts about walking round the coast of Britain, the one thing that made me stop and listen was the all-important phrase, "I believe God has spoken to me." I didn't sense that Gary had an agenda, or wanted to make a name for himself. Instead, he carried in his heart a genuine love and care for people, and now he was called to communicate this, in a greater and perhaps more creative way. Here was a young man who was fit, healthy, great with people, and outwardly possessed of all the qualities one would need for such a venture.

But it was as some of us, as leaders, watched the vision develop, and had to talk through the implications, that realization began to dawn regarding the degree of over-all support and commitment he needed to meet such a challenge. So it was in those early days that I was reminded of the above quote, and understood that Gary's vision – if it was to be outworked – would need all of Swindoll's ingredients!

To a degree I was able to take a back seat, but I kept careful watch as Gary – with the help of a number of others – put some shape and structure onto what he was carrying in his heart. There are many whom I could thank for all those months of hard work, both before and during the walk, but one I feel I do need to personally acknowledge is Vincent Oliver, part of the pastoral team in South Kent Community Church. He worked tirelessly on Gary's behalf, both in the preparation and the ongoing co-ordination of the walk.

I believe it is no exaggeration to say that the church was 100% behind Gary both before and during his walk, supporting financially, verbally encouraging and – most importantly – praying for him.

To have been with many others, on the morning when Gary set off, and to have had the opportunity to walk at different stages with him on his journey, was a tremendous joy and privilege. But to have been there at the end, with an even greater number of people welcoming him back to Kent, re-confirmed for me that God really had spoken to Gary, all that time ago.

Graham Coombs *(senior leader)*

Isle of Wight

Gary and I caught the ferry to the Isle of Wight at 9.45 a.m. on 27th January. I had bought some chocolate bars, attaching scriptures and information about Gary's walk to them. We attempted to give them out on the ferry, but met with a lot of resistance. People refused them, but offered us money, which was not the reaction we wanted! We were then asked to stop, because we had not got permission from the crew.

After a bus ride from Yarmouth to The Needles, we began walking along the coastal path. It was a really cold day, but the scenery was stunning. We met a Brazilian called William, who wanted to walk with us. Gary interviewed him on camcorder, about whether he had a faith and what was the purpose of life.

Near The Needles, we had the opportunity to pray for a lady whose sister was suffering from cancer. She had twin granddaughters in her care. This really touched me, as I also have twin girls. William parted company with us and – at the bottom of a hill with Tennyson's memorial at the top – we prayed for a couple. The lady was going to have an operation to remove a rib, which is a bit unusual to say the least.

Gary felt the Holy Spirit was urging him to climb up to the memorial, and sure enough – at the top we met a man called Alan, who was out of work. He seemed very grateful that we offered to pray for him.

In the beautiful thatched church of Freshwater we prayed for the youth of the village.

By now lunch was calling, so we went looking for food. All we could find was a tea room. Gary was probably hoping for chips or something, but the menu was a little more refined. We enjoyed pancakes with ham and cheese, a cup of tea with scones, jam and cream, plus a good conversation with two ladies, and left with full stomachs.

We talked together about our fathers, and I shared how I felt I wanted more love from mine. We prayed about it. Soon afterwards my time with Gary came to an end, as I had to catch the bus back to Yarmouth and then return to Hythe, Kent. I really enjoyed my day with Gary. In fact I felt uplifted. The biggest challenge from the day was – "When was the last time you asked to pray for someone that you don't know, right then and there?"

The very next morning, my father and stepmother unexpectedly paid one of their rare visits. Alison and I asked if we could pray with them. It was a little embarrassing, and a struggle, but we went ahead. I doubt if I would have done that before walking with Gary.

Richard M

Postscript

God is still at work in me

Throughout the two years it has taken us to prepare this book, I served my church as youth pastor and really enjoyed it. However, the passion for prayer has never left me, and although I shall miss regular direct interaction with a group of young people really going for it with God, I feel called to pray. Thankfully for me, the church has recognized this, and together we are now travelling on a new journey – wait for it ... I now get paid to pray!

Of course, it is not as simple as that, because it is not just about me! Along with the leaders of our church we want to mobilise prayer in the area more, and see other churches working together to see this take place. Different denominations can feel separated by numerous opposing theologies, but what I love about prayer is that it is so non-threatening and potentially unifying. I only set out on this new role at the start of 2008, so I by no means feel like an expert and am wide open to input from others who share my prayer-obsession. So, if you are interested and full of ideas, I would like to hear from you on skcic@btconnect.com

"Ask and it will be given ... " (Matthew 7:7)

We hope you enjoyed reading this New Wine book.
For details of other New Wine books
and a range of 2,000 titles from other
Word and Spirit publishers visit our website:
www.newwineministries.co.uk
email: newwine@xalt.co.uk